*All for the Love
of
Our Lady*

Patricia Brookes

TRICORN
BOOKS
www.tricornbooks.co.uk

All for the Love of Our Lady
Published by Tricorn Books

Design © 131 Design Ltd
www.131design.org

Text © Patricia Brookes

Patricia Brookes has asserted her right under the Copyright, Design and Patents Act 1988 to be identified as the author of this work. This book is sold subject to the conditions that it shall not by way of trade or otherwise, be lent, resold, hired out or otherwise circulated without the publisher's prior consent in any form of binding or cover other than that in which it is published and without a similar condition including this condition being imposed on the subsequent purchaser.

ISBN 978-0-9568743-7-5

Published 2011 by
Tricorn Books
a trading name of
131 Design Ltd
131 High Street
Old Portsmouth
PO1 2HW

TRICORN
BOOKS
www.tricornbooks.co.uk

*All for the Love
of
Our Lady*

Patricia Brookes

Contents

The Early Years	1
Childhood	8
Faith	11
Growing Up	16
Working Girl	29
Roy	31
Australia	35
Married Life	45
Visitors	53
Working On the Oilrigs	58
Buying Our Own Home	59
Our Second Child	62
Journey Home	67
Back Home	71
Our Own Home	77
Illness	82
Reunited with My Father	86
Frank's Death	90
Lourdes	96
Back from Lourdes	103
My Miracle Baby	108
Legion of Mary	114
Driving Lessons	122

Working for Our Lady	130
Hospital Visitations	143
Home-to-Home	158
Caroline	165
Living with Grief	172
Pilgrimages	177
Business Problems	181
Our Parish Church	192
Missionaries	199
My Retirement	205
Celebrations	208
The Conclusion	213
Acknowledgements	217

The Early Years

On the night before I was born, when my mother was in labour, Birmingham was under heavy bombing. It was the beginning of World War II and the year of the Battle of Britain. So, on Sunday morning, 1st September 1940, I came into the world in my grandparents' house at 179 George Road, Erdington. Shortly after I was born, my mother bundled me up into a tallboy drawer and carried me down to the air-raid shelter at the far end of the back garden and there we stayed every night for a week. Mom later told me that all morning the church bells had been ringing calling everyone to prayer and they've been ringing out ever since, as we have been called to prayer so many times.

At the age of two weeks I was baptised Patricia Kathleen Murray in the Catholic Church. My father was away in the war, not fighting the enemy but entertaining the troops abroad, mainly in the Middle East, as part of the Entertainments National Service Association (ENSA). I remember him telling us that Tommy Cooper, the comedian and magician, was also in his group, and my dad was with him in Cairo when he bought his first red Fez hat with the tassel on, which he always wore when he appeared on stage or TV.

For the first six years of my life I hardly saw my father, though he did come home on leave a few times, on each occasion leaving my mother pregnant. After the war was over, he was back home and Mom was expecting baby number four. By the time I was seven years old I was the eldest of four children; next to me was my brother John, then came my sister Carole, and now baby Francis, whom we called Frankie.

The winter of 1947/48 was very severe, the worst on record, with thick snow for months. When Frankie was being born it was my job to go and get the midwife to come and deliver the baby at home; she only lived a few streets away. I didn't even have time to get dressed. I was woken up by my grandmother saying, "Just put your coat on over your pyjamas and go quickly". She had been with my mom all night. I flew out of the house, still half asleep, trudging along in the snow saying my prayers on the way, asking God to look after my mom and not to let her die. The midwife was an elderly lady who rode a sit-up-and-beg bike with a large black leather bag on the handlebars. How slow she was peddling; I was able to keep up with her by running alongside.

As usual, my father wasn't at home – he travelled around seeking work in clubs and theatres and very often had to stay out of town overnight – but shortly after Frankie was born, dad left for good. Mom said that the army had changed him and he was not the same man she had married. Being a sergeant in the army had made him more bossy and bigheaded; apparently he wanted to follow his career, which was taking off with lots of bookings on the stage and at workingmen's clubs. He would sing and yodel and tell jokes, and being a handsome Irishman, everyone loved him and told him that he was even better than Joseph Locke, the famous tenor, as he sang just like him. The women flocked round him and he lapped that up, consequently he was tempted to be unfaithful. There were lots of rows and fights at home; mom was very jealous of his lifestyle while she was home alone looking after us four children.

One day, when he was still at home, she pawned all his best clothes so he couldn't go out to a concert and his best shoes were put in the dustbin, but that didn't stop him; he borrowed what he needed and went. In fact that's when he went for good, because he was so angry.

Until he came home from the war we had all been living at my grandparents' house, but we had recently moved into a rented house, which mom had a hard time keeping up. It was a terrible struggle. My dad was supposed to pay maintenance money to the court each week for our keep but he never kept up with the payments. Each Monday I'd go to town with my mom to collect it but the clerk of the court would say: "Sorry Mrs Murray, nothing today". The court tried to trace his whereabouts but he wasn't to be found, because he'd move about, staying in different lodging houses in different towns. All we knew was that he'd originally gone up north to Sheffield. Mom went up there once to track him down but was told that he had moved to York, so she got on another train and found him lodging in a house with a group of theatricals. He told her that he had fallen on hard times ever since he was involved in a bad car accident, disfiguring his face and losing his good looks: he could no longer get work. Mom said it was judgement on him for what he had done to us and it served him right.

There was no Social Security in those days and no help from anywhere except for free dinners and milk at school; we would go up for second helpings if we could get them because there was so little food at home.

When the gas man and the electric man came to empty the meters, instead of finding it full of shillings, they would find metal discs the size of a shilling. When mom didn't have a shilling for the meter and we were either in the dark or with no gas to cook on, she took the lid off the cocoa tin and with a strong pair of scissors she cut a disc the same size as a shilling piece. She put that in the meter and – hey presto – we had light. By the time the meters were due to be emptied, she somehow had to find the equivalent in real money to give to the collectors in exchange for the discs. Those men got used to giving the discs back if she paid up, and you could bet she used them over and over again. Sometimes if the gasman came early and caught her by surprise, she didn't have the money: so we all had to keep quiet and pretend we were out.

Once, mom bought herself a fur coat from the second-hand shop, and when she got home she found some silver coins in the pocket. That night we were sent to the off-licence shop for bottles of pop and crisps and sweets as a treat with the money. We didn't have many sweets and we were so happy that you'd think we had won the 'pools', but when we got to the shop, the man said, "These are foreign coins – French," and chased us out. We didn't know, but our mom must have known and hoped the shopkeeper wouldn't notice. That was another disappointment for us children.

One thing about never having sweets was that we all had perfect teeth with no cavities. I can only remember going to the dentist once as a child to have a tooth out and was put to sleep with gas. It was very frightening for me, and from that day I would never agree to having a general anaesthetic for dental work. As an adult, I once had to have eight teeth out at the same time and insisted that I had Novocaine injections instead, but afterwards my face became very swollen with Novocaine poisoning.

We used to collect empty pop bottles and take them back to the shop for a few pennies and instead of taking the bus home from school we'd walk miles to save the fare, so we could have an ice-cream on the way home. Fish and chips were a treat, and on the rare occasions that we had some we always asked the chip-shop man for a free bag of scratchings, which were tiny bits of batter off the fish.

On a Saturday, grandad used to go to the fish market at the Birmingham Bull Ring, and bring back whelks, cockles, mussels and periwinkles; I loved shellfish and got great enjoyment from sitting with a pin and picking out the periwinkle from inside the shell. Another thing that the pin came in use for was when we managed to get a pomegranate, also a real treat.

You may think that I'm always talking about food, but that was all we had to look forward to in those days. Even a toilet roll was a luxury. We would have to cut up newspaper into squares and hang the squares on a piece of string on a nail in the outside toilet. It was educational to sit in the toilet reading snippets of news from the *News of the World* or the *Daily Mirror*. There were no indoor toilets, and during the winter months it was so cold that you spent as little time as you could in there.

Occasionally we had comics to read, *The Dandy* and *The Beano* being the favourites, and we used to swap them with other children for ones that we hadn't read. I remember collecting the cigarette cards that were inside my grandfather's and uncle's cigarette packets. We had thousands of them by the time we had swapped some for ones we didn't have. We put them into sets which would be worth quite a bit today if we had saved them, as would the foreign stamps in stamp albums that I avidly collected. I don't know what became of them – I think they got lost during one of our house-moves.

Mom lived in the second-hand shops, always trying to keep us clean and tidy. The only time we had any new clothes was at Easter when she got a provident cheque from a loan company that you could spend in certain shops to buy us a new coat or shoes and she'd then struggle to meet the weekly payments for the rest of the year.

Such was life, but we weren't the only family living on the bread-line – everyone was poor during and shortly after the war. People shared and helped each other then; there were good neighbours and you could leave your door open or unlocked without the fear of having things stolen, not that we had much to steal. Children were safe to play outside without worrying about paedophiles and kidnappers; I feel sorry for the children of today who are shut up in the house watching TV or playing on computers, not having the joy of playing outside all day.

We had *Daily Mail* shoes that were hand-outs from the government for poor families, they always had the D.M. initials on the side though and I used to get a razorblade and try to scrape those letters off and camouflage it with black shoe polish. We lived on hand-me-down clothes from the family next door, where the children were a little older than us; if it wasn't for good grandparents we really would have starved. We went to bed many a night hungry with old army coats on the bed to keep us warm. We all went to school at the Erdington Abbey Catholic School.

My mom got a cleaner's job at St Agnes's Convent opposite where we went to school, taking Frankie with her in his pram. Her working day finished just before we came out of school and she would pick us up. She did her best but, boy, was it hard, washing our school clothes every night and trying to dry them by the fire overnight for the next day; we may have been poor but we were clean. We never knew what it was like to have sweets or fruit except when I went to see my nan who saved me her ration of one banana a month, and on Thursday nights, when my grandfather – who worked at Dunlop's as a paint sprayer – called on his way home from work with a bag of sweets as it was payday, and we'd look forward to that.

He used to do the Football Pools every week and lived in hope of winning the £75,000. He was always promising us what he would buy us if his Pools came in. He used to say to me, "Patty my darling, I'm going to give you a college education," and I would believe him, but when I told my grandmother what he had said she would laugh and say, "The only college education you will get off him, love, is in the College Arms pub up the road".

He liked a drink and came home drunk every night, singing up the road, *'Oh, Oh Antonio'*, or *'Lily of Laguna'*, because his name was Tony and nan's name was Lily. The neighbours could set their clocks every night by him singing on his way home from the Brookvale pub.

My grandfather could tap-dance just as well as Fred Astaire, and I've been told when he'd had a drink he entertained everyone at the pub by dancing on top of the tables. He was a slightly built man, very thin, always smoking Woodbine cigarettes. They called them 'Coffin Nails' and I hated the smell of them; even his clothes smelled of cigarettes and if it wasn't cigarettes it was beer he would smell of. But he was a good man, so inoffensive and very easy-going.

Childhood

We lived on broken promises all our childhood; it was always what we might have, if mom could get the money…. but this never happened. I looked forward all the week to being able to go to the 'pictures' at the weekend, only to be disappointed because we couldn't afford it. There was no television then, so the radio was our main entertainment. We didn't have many toys except a whip-and-top that I used to colour with chalks round the top; we had many happy hours of fun whipping it and keeping it spinning for ages in the street. We never had a bike either, but one Christmas I was given a scooter and was so thrilled scooting along the footpath. It was safe to play in the horse-road then because there was hardly any traffic, except for the milk cart and the baker's van, which was drawn by an old carthorse, with his hay bag round his neck; we always saved him a carrot.

As time went on, mom had men-friends and she started going out to the pub with them; there were infidelities on both sides now, and mom and dad got divorced.

I was about 11 years old and had just moved to senior school when I came home from school one day, just half an hour later than my siblings, to find the house locked up and all our furniture thrown out into the back garden. We had been evicted for not paying the rent. I just sat on the back doorstep and sobbed. The lady next door heard me and popped her head over the fence saying: "They have all gone to your nan and grandad's, love." So mom and us four children were all put up in nan's front room downstairs, and later that night my grandad went with his handcart (the one he carried all his paint-pots on when he decorated people's houses), to collect all our bits and pieces from our house. We were to stay at nan's for three years.

My grandmother was a saintly woman who, apart from putting up with us lot living there, also had her three sons (mom's brothers) back home from the war; they were all in their 20s and 30s. They had been in the three different services – one in the Army, one in the Navy , and the other in the Royal Air Force. Now they were all back home and in work, so there was always food on the table, either a rabbit stew on the stove, or a nice cooked dinner every night. My nan was a good cook. I loved to get the big toasting fork and cut a thick slice of bread and do myself some toast by the open coal fire, then spread lard or dripping on it that we got from the Sunday roast. Food tasted so much better then, and we were always hungry.

My grandfather and uncles used to come home drunk every night from the pub, and it was one long round of fights, drunken brawls and arguments living there, not a good environment for children to grow up in. They were gamblers too – as well as betting on horses every day and doing the Pools every week, they would bet on anything and everything. They even bet with each other as to who had answered a quiz question correctly and would write to the 'Old Codgers' column in the *Daily Mirror* to find out who was correct. Coming from a family of boozers and gamblers and seeing what a mug's game it was, with never having anything worthwhile in life, I learned to steer clear of such pursuits.

One night, when everyone was out at the pub and I was left to look after the younger ones, we were all in bed when I heard someone force the front door and break in. I thought we were being burgled; I could hear doors slamming and cupboards being opened as if they were looking for something. I was terrified, expecting us to be murdered in our beds. It was the only time in my life that I trembled and shook with fear. I told the other children to hide under the beds and they started to cry; the burglar must have heard them crying and left. As it happens, it wasn't a burglar; it was one of mom's ex-boyfriends, blind drunk and looking for her. When she found out what happened, she took him to court for breaking and entering, and for terrorising us children. He told the court that he didn't break in, he didn't have to as mom had left the key on a piece of string dangling behind the letter-box – all he'd had to do was put his hand inside and reach for the key. Mom was livid because it was all lies which he'd told on oath. She shouted out in court, "liar, you just perjured yourself and will go to hell now." Shortly after that we heard he had died of cancer, and as a child I often wondered if he did go to hell and get his just desserts for frightening us so much.

Faith

*M*y grandmother gave me her 'Love for Our Lady'. I loved my nan and became very close to her. Actually, you could say we were all granny-reared, because she cared for us more than mom did. She suffered very badly with arthritis in her legs and was crippled with it, but being the good Catholic woman that she was, she still walked up two long hills to Mass on Sunday morning to St. Johns and I went with her. Sometimes I would meet her coming back along the road from shopping, carrying heavy bags and crying because she was in so much pain. I'd help her carry her bags; she never complained. I used to think she was a Saint. She was always praying and asking Our Lady to help her. I can still hear her saying: "Trust in Our Lady, Patty, because she will never let you down." She used to tell me about her younger years when she was in the Legion of Mary at church: helping the priest, doing the cleaning, washing the altar cloths and vestments, visiting the sick at home and in hospitals. I was very interested in that and thought when I grew up I would like to do that too.

Mom was a Catholic and sent us all to a Catholic school but was always too busy to go to Mass herself: after getting us ready to go, she stayed at home to prepare the Sunday dinner. Mom had her own idea of God, how He knew what she was doing and that He understood if she didn't go to church. She did pray though and taught us to pray, as there were lots of occasions when we needed to pray for things. She used to say to us when we needed something, "Well, I haven't got it, and you haven't got a father, so ask your Heavenly Father for it." We learnt from a very early age to trust in God's providence.

Every night at 7pm we all had to kneel down and say the family rosary. This was something that had been started by a well-known priest, Father Patrick Peyton, known as the 'Rosary Priest', whose slogan was: 'The family that prays together, stays together'. Mom said that meant that we would always stay close to one another and stick together no matter what. We would always share with each other too, so if one of us had any good fortune we must share it with the family. Whatever was happening each night, we couldn't go out before saying the Rosary together.

At school during the Rosary Crusade, every child in my class was asked to draw and paint a picture depicting the Rosary, and the winning picture would be pinned up on the wall of the school corridor. Some drew a picture of a large rosary, others a picture of St Dominic receiving the rosary from Our Lady, but I drew a picture of our family kneeling down with the rosary in our hands; mom, me, John, Carol and Frank, all saying the family rosary together. I didn't think it was good enough to win the competition but, surprise, surprise, guess who won first prize? I was so proud to see my drawing hanging on the corridor wall. I remember winning a huge box of chocolates but couldn't open them until we were all together and could all have an equal share. My Uncle Bob saw the chocolates and said we shouldn't open them at all, as he could raffle them off at the pub that night and make some money. With that, I quickly took the cellophane wrapper off and opened the box, because I knew that the proceeds would only go on beer.

Throughout all our lives after that, we shared everything with each other. The family rosary went on for years, and one night mom came in with a framed picture of Our Lady of Fatima and hung it up on the wall of the lounge. In that picture there were three children kneeling down: two girls and a boy, saying the rosary like us. Our Frank went up to the picture saying, "that's Pat, that's John and that's Carol, but where am I?" He was so upset about not being in the picture, but of course, later on we learned that Our Lady appeared to just three children, Lucia, Jacinta and Francisco We learnt about it at school: apparently the two youngest of the children died in childhood but the oldest, Lucia, was now a nun in Portugal and lived to a great old age. It fascinated me to know that she had really seen Our Lady, and I wished it could have been me. Our Lady was supposed to have given secrets to the children, and one was to be given to the Pope.

Incidentally, my father never sent us a birthday or Christmas card; he completely cut himself off from us, so when I realised that my prayers were working and it was possible to live on miracles, this spurred me on to pray all the more, not only for myself but also for others. If anyone was sick or in trouble, or had died, out would come my rosary, because it is a wholesome thing to do to pray for the dead: the Holy Souls in purgatory couldn't help themselves but we could help, with our prayers. I also prayed for simple everyday things: "Lord, don't let me be late for school again", "make the bus come soon," and "help me get better from this bad chest."

I wasn't a very strong girl; I was pale, thin and undernourished and suffered from bouts of bronchitis and chest infections. The school doctor sent me to an open-air school for a month, where every day I had sunray treatment to build me up.

When I was about nine, I was running down a steep slope and couldn't stop in time before crashing into a brick wall, hitting my nose on the corner of the wall. I ended up with a broken nose and two black eyes, but to my knowledge I never went to the doctor's. Mom didn't believe in doctors. I think deep down she was afraid of them, especially if we looked battered, just in case the authorities were called in thinking she was cruel to us: we might be taken away from her and put into care. She used to say a woman on her own had to be careful because she was vulnerable, so no doctors. Consequently, I went through life with a diverted septum blocking my nose and hampering my breathing, although it wasn't visible externally.

When I was about ten years old, I was due to make my first Holy Communion. All my girlfriends at school were excited about getting lovely white dresses for the occasion, but we couldn't afford one. I was getting desperate as the day drew closer. I prayed really hard to Our Lady and God to work a miracle, and find me a dress and veil – otherwise I was lost.

The day before I was to make my Holy Communion, my mother took me to all the second-hand shops in the area, looking for a dress to wear, which of course had to be white. I was thinking: well, if we manage to find a dress, I doubt if we will find a veil as well. We had tried dozens of shops, all to no avail. By about 4:45pm, with 15 minutes before closing time, we found ourselves in the last second-hand shop and it was my last chance to get anything. I started to think I'd have to pretend to be ill tomorrow and not go to school at all because I had nothing to wear. When my mother asked the assistant if she had a white dress to fit me, she looked doubtful and went into the back stockroom to search, having found nothing in the shop.

I was praying: "Please Lord, let her come out with one," but no luck.

"Sorry," she said, and my heart sank once again. Just then a woman customer, who was browsing through the clothes' rail said to us, "Wait a minute, I have a Communion dress and veil at home from my daughter's first Holy Communion last year. If you would like to come home with me you can have it. I think it will fit."

'Thank you God, you didn't let me down'. It did fit and the next day I looked as good as any other girl in my beautiful dress and veil. It had been a little grubby when we got it, but Mom had washed it in bleach and spent all night drying it by the fire, until it came up as good as new and no-one was any the wiser. Yet another miracle wrought by prayer. There were oh so many other occasions, where only a miracle would solve the problem, but I did learn that nothing was impossible with God.

In my younger days I was a timid nervous person who worried a lot, until I read in the Bible, 'Cast all your cares on the Lord for He knows exactly what you need, even before you ask for it,' and 'Seek ye first the kingdom of God and all these things will be added unto you'.

Years later another wonderful book I read was *'The Imitation of Christ'*, by Thomas à Kempis. In it, I read that in order to bear the weight of big crosses, we first have to experience smaller ones. God knows the future, and He moulds us and helps us carry our crosses, making us stronger each time to overcome the problems they represent. In other words, 'what don't kill us, makes us stronger', as the saying goes. It is like having the measles or the chickenpox as a child, which gives us immunity in later life, because we are able to fight the disease: likewise, getting over smaller hurdles strengthens us for bigger ones, and He never gives us a cross we cannot carry.

Growing Up

I remember we could never go on school trips without a uniform, and once John's teacher took him to Lewis's the big department store in Corporation Street and bought him the school uniform out of her own pocket so he could go. My mother went into school to thank her. She knew that Mrs Dell had taken a shine to our John and he liked her too, but Mrs Dell told mom that she felt so sorry for John when he told her that his mom didn't love him. Mom's excuse was that 'his dad has left us, and John is the man of the family now so he's got to toughen up and I'm not going to mollycoddle him.'

But in actual fact, none of us were mollycoddled. I can't remember ever sitting on her lap, having a cuddle or her kissing us. All her life, even up to her death at 86, she would turn her head away if you went to kiss her. I asked her once about why she did that and she said: "Well, when you don't get any love as a child yourself, you have difficulty in giving love as an adult." She confessed that she never loved any man, not even my father with whom she had had four children. She said she had only married him to get away from home. She often said that her own mom hadn't loved her, but had only loved her brothers. I couldn't believe that because my nan was a loving woman and always showed me such affection. I could only think mom must have been a very naughty child and caused nan such anguish. It was true: she even ran away from home once. She didn't love her brothers as she should have done, and I don't think they loved her very much either; certainly they weren't as close as a family should be. Mom showed no emotion when they died either – it was so strange and I couldn't understand it.

Once when mom had said something hurtful to my grandmother, as she often did, leaving her in tears, I went to comfort nan and she said: "Patty, your mom has a heart of gold but a very wicked tongue, and a jealous nature." I knew that to be true, but why? What's made her like that? I wondered about that all my life, and one day, when I was 38, I discovered the reason that made me understand her better, which I will disclose later in this book.

Our childhood wasn't all bad; there were some happy times too. We used to play with all the neighbour's children, and pass many happy hours playing hide and seek, leap-frog, kick the can, hopscotch and hand-stands. Sometimes I borrowed an old curtain and put on a show in the back garden, singing and dancing and doing turns. We would go apple scrumping and pinching all the strawberries out of grandad's allotment. He grew lots of vegetables including cabbages, and I would spend hours collecting all the Cabbage White caterpillars off them to stop them eating holes in the leaves. I used to find lots of Woolly Bear caterpillars too, but I think I was fighting a losing battle, because the next day there would be just as many again. There used to be hundreds of butterflies when I was a child, and I'd try to catch them with a fishing-net. Things like that teach you patience.

It was my job to go into the 'horse-road' with a bucket and shovel to collect horse-manure for grandad's rhubarb. It really worked too; his rhubarb plants were huge. Nan used to make lovely pies and crumbles with them.

The man next door kept racing-pigeons and we would sneak in and steal the pigeon eggs. We had a rabbit named Floppy because of his floppy ears. When we couldn't get carrots or greens to give him to eat, we could always find plenty of dandelion leaves out of the garden. Mom used to save all the potato peelings for him, too. She boiled them and mashed porridge oats in with them; it smelt so good I could have eaten it myself. He loved it, especially when it was still warm, and he grew really fat. One day he went missing – someone must have left the latch of the hutch undone and he got out. I always had my suspicions that Floppy had gone into the stew-pot but we weren't told. I remember asking:

"Is this rabbit in the dinner?"

"No it's chicken," was the reply, but the only time we ever had chicken was at Christmas.

We also had goldfish in a little round bowl, but they never lasted long. We got them off the rag-and-bone man who used to come round for old clothes, and we would find him what we could in exchange for a goldfish in a plastic bag of water. Sometimes instead of goldfish we got a fluffy yellow baby chick and we would keep it in a box by the fire, but they never lived long either.

I remember a visit from my great-uncle, my grandfather's brother, who had served in the army in India. He gave me a peacock's feather – apparently there are lots of peacocks in India. I had never seen a real one before, only in picture books, and I was fascinated at the beautiful colours shaping into a coloured eye at the top. I took it to school to show the class. The teacher was pleased about that and kept it in the school, but I never got it back.

My great-uncle had married an Indian lady who wore beautiful Sari dresses, and they had a son about my age. It was the first time I had ever met an Indian boy with dark skin and – confusing him with Africans in the jungle – I asked him if they wore grass skirts where he came from. He said, "No" and seemed quite annoyed with me.

My best friend lived next door and we did everything together. We used to sit on the back doorstep eating pieces of HP sauce. The HP sauce factory was only down the road and it gave off wafts of smells. My nan would say, "All that vinegar will dry your blood up". If it wasn't brown sauce on the bread, it would be butter with sugar sprinkled on it; jam was a luxury.

When I was about 10-years old at Junior School, we were taught by nuns. Sister Mary Leonie talked about martyrs in Religious Education one day, and about people who had died for their faith. She spoke about Christians in other parts of the world who were being persecuted and killed and how these people were all martyrs, and went straight to Heaven. She concluded by saying, "I wonder how many of us could be martyrs, if Communists with guns broke into this classroom today, asking 'who would die for their religion; how many of you would stand up?'"

That question haunted me as to what I would do if it really happened. As I had a vivid imagination, I would keep a close eye on the classroom door in case it did open.

Nan's kitchen was a haven for me. I can picture her house now: in fact when my brother came over to visit from Australia I took him on a trip down memory lane to where we were born and grew up. It's funny how you always imagined it bigger as a child: we used to play hide-and-seek in that front garden, but now it seems so small to us. Nan's house was a nice semi-detached house with bay windows at the front. In between the houses was an entry with two gates at the end, one opening up into nan's backyard, with a French door to the lounge and the kitchen door and window. As you opened the door into the kitchen (where everyone gathered), there was a gas stove behind the door and, next to that, a deep white crock sink with a draining board with a curtain across the cupboard below where all the pots and pans and dishes were kept, then came a large round boiler up the corner, where all the washing was done on a Monday – no washing machines in those days!

Just a big wooden stick called a 'maid', to swirl the clothes round while they were being boiled in the water, and on wash days, if I wasn't at school, I helped to wring the clothes out by putting them through a big wooden mangle in the back yard, then hanging them out on the long clothes line in the big back garden. Next to the boiler was the fireplace with the black iron range with a coal fire; we had to polish that range with lead polish and it used to come up like new. I remember when we were running short of coal, my grandfather mixed peat, (clods of earth) with coal dust and would burn those on the fire.

On the other side of the fireplace was an alcove with a shelf halfway up the wall. A radio sat on the shelf, and underneath that was another gingham check curtain on a wire across the alcove. Behind that curtain was a cardboard box with a mother cat and four or five kittens in it; that box was never empty because we had a lot of cats and one of them was always having kittens. I used to play with the cats, teasing them with balls of wool or a rabbit's tail on a piece of string.

With no television, the radio was our main entertainment. I listened to the radio a lot; there was always lovely music playing (I especially loved opera and classical music), and we all enjoyed the plays and serials: *Educating Archie, Dick Barton Special Agent* and the *Just William* series. Below the radio, next to the fire, was an old leatherette armchair and us kids used to fight to sit there by the fire in the winter if none of the grown-ups were there.

Against the long wall opposite the sink was a large wooden table that was scrubbed every day to keep it clean, and above that were two Sacred Heart pictures on the wall signed by the priest when he came to bless the house years ago; those pictures consoled me in many a sad moment. On the opposite wall to the fireplace, by the back door, was a bookcase. We didn't have many books unless we went to the lending library, but what we did have we would read over and over again. I loved books – still do.

Next to the electric light bulb hanging from the ceiling was a flypaper that always had lots of dead flies stuck to it. We also had gas lamps on the wall that were used when the electricity money ran out in the meter; they gave good light but the gas mantles were very delicate and flimsy, and kept burning into holes. I was forever being sent to the corner shop with a penny to buy new ones, I used to run every-ones errands.

My grandfather would come home from the pub on a Sunday afternoon and sit facing the Sacred Heart pictures on the wall while he had his dinner. Ashamed of being drunk, he used to turn the pictures to the wall saying: "You two can stop looking at me like that, can't a man have a drink?" Sometimes he fell asleep in the armchair while waiting for his dinner, and for a laugh nan would wipe gravy round his mouth and whiskers. When he woke up saying, "I'll have my dinner now, my darling," nan would say, "don't be daft, you've already had it – look, you still have some round your moustache." And he'd believe her. We all giggled but thought what a shame it was, and how cruel.

Nan was a great knitter and taught me how to knit, and it wasn't long before I was doing big things like cardigans for myself. One day, I was trying to finish a cardigan to wear the next day on an outing, but as night came I could see that I would never finish the last sleeve in time and so went to bed with it unfinished. The next morning, there was the cardigan all ready for me to wear; my grandmother had stayed up half the night knitting and finishing it for me.

We each had our jobs to do: John chopping fire-wood, one of us cleaning all the shoes, another cleaning the windows, or polishing the front doorstep with Red Cardinal polish and the doorknocker and letterbox with Brasso metal polish. Nan took pride in her home and always kept it nice but used to complain to my grandad that, given he was a painter and decorator with his signboard up on the wall advertising his trade, her windows were the worst in the street.

The job I used to hate most was fetching coal from the coal yard. Every week my brother John and I took it in turns to get the old pram from the back yard to collect the coal in. Off we went with the words: "Here's the money and don't get your clothes dirty." How on earth could you not get your clothes dirty handling coal? We always came back looking like chimney sweeps, covered in coal-dust, or looking like Uncle Tony who worked down the mines. That coal yard was situated where Spaghetti Junction in Birmingham is now. It used to be called Salford Bridge.

My favourite hobby was fishing. We lived opposite a large park with a big pool full of fish; anglers were always dotted along the bank every day. I used to get a long cane from the runner bean patch in the garden, find a piece of strong wire, bend it round into a loop and attach it to the end of the cane. Then, I would get an old nylon stocking, sew the top around the wire, cut the stocking into the length of a fishing net and sew it up; it made a great fishing net. To put the fish in when caught, I used a jam-jar or large pickled onion jar, tying string around the rim to make a handle to carry it with, and just like Huckleberry Finn, I'd spend hours in the park by the pond. I became champion gudgeon catcher because I knew where all their hiding holes were along the bank. Other times, I took stale bread to feed the ducks and swans, and when I was 14 I learnt to row the rowing boats on the lake as good as any lad. I think I was a bit of a tomboy in my early teens. The summers and the days seemed so much longer then: I used to take some sandwiches and a bottle of tea and sit on the bank under a leafy tree, daydreaming of what I'd be when I grew up.

One day when I was about 11 years old we were all so hungry but we didn't have anything to eat in the house: mom said she didn't know what to do. As it happened our next-door neighbour, Mrs Williams, who was elderly, had gone away for a week to stay with her daughter and left a house key with mom, to look after the place for her, and perhaps do a bit of cleaning for her while she was away. Suddenly mom shot up with the key: "I know what I'll do, I'll see what Mrs Williams has got in her pantry and borrow it and put it back before she gets back at the weekend."

So off she went next door while we all sat waiting in anticipation with our tummies rumbling, wondering what niceties she would find and bring back for our tea. Back she came with a brown paper bag.

"What did you find, mom?" we all shouted, excited. "Well," she said, "would you believe it, her pantry is as bare as ours. All I could find was a few onions and some Oxo cubes. I will make some onion soup and you can dip this bread in it."

Well, she did, and we sat eating it, but I remember saying: "mom, I don't like it, this is horrible." She replied, "Get it down you – it's all we have got, or you will go to bed hungry again."

Afterwards we would all say our prayers thanking God for food in our bellies but secretly, I complained to Him that next time could He send something nicer, with maybe a cake for afterwards.

The weekend came, Mrs Williams returned from her holiday and came round for her spare key. As she was leaving she turned to mom and said: "Thanks for looking after the house, Lilly. Oh, and by the way, what did you do with the daffodil bulbs out of my pantry?"

We all went quiet. I put my hand over my mouth; we couldn't say that we had eaten them, so mom told her: "Oh, Patty has planted them for you in the front garden under the window." Every spring Mrs Williams would stand with her hands on her hips saying: "I can't see those daffodils coming up Patty. You must have planted them upside down." I got the blame for that. Years later I learnt that daffodils were poisonous. I read in the newspaper that an old man made the same mistake and put daffodil bulbs in his stew instead of onions and it killed him: we had done the same and lived to tell the tale.

One night when we were saying the family rosary, there was a torrential storm outside with floods in the back garden, which ran down to the back door as we were on a slope, our drain was blocked up and the water started to overflow and came into the house under the door. I was so nervous when I saw the water gushing in that my Hail Mary's got louder and louder. The living room was flooded and we were paddling in it, and there was our mom and John outside with the poker trying to unblock the drain to allow the water to go down. Finally it subsided, but we had a lot of cleaning up to do. The lino on the floor was sopping wet and took weeks to dry out, and we had to throw away the homemade hearthrug as it began to smell. I was sad about that, as I had made it out of bits of woollen material and an old sack, using a bodkin hook. I tried to make some sort of pattern out of different colours and it had done the job of making the room look more homely.

Looking back, I'm grateful for my poor childhood because it taught me lots of things which have seen me in good stead over the years, like knowing how to make-do and mend, and not to be wasteful. I learned how to repair things. I could sew and knit and make my own clothes; I could make curtains and cushions, and even mend shoes. My grandad had an old iron last that could be adjusted to any size, and whenever our soles and heels wore into holes, I'd watch him mend the shoes with a piece of leather. Sometimes he managed to get rubber soles and heels, and he'd stick them on with glue. We just couldn't afford new ones. When I think what we all have now, so many dozens of pairs; children today don't know they are born. I could change a plug, I learnt how to put a washer on a leaky tap and was quite resourceful and wouldn't be beaten: where there was a will there was a way, and I had a strong will.

Mom became more depressed with the situation at home,

with never having any money and trying to cope with everything alone. She threatened us all with putting us into Father Hudson's Children's Home in Coleshill, saying she couldn't keep us. She gave Frankie away for 12 months to an old aunt and uncle who couldn't have any children, and they wanted to adopt him, but when they came with the papers for mom to sign, she changed her mind. She took him back but became neurotic and threatened suicide.

I couldn't concentrate on my lessons at school because before I left home each morning, mom would say to me: "I won't be here when you get home from school because I will be dead." She said she would either put her head in the gas oven, or if she didn't have enough money for the gas, she would throw herself in the park pool. There were undercurrents in that pool that dragged you down, and many people, even sailors who were good swimmers, had drowned in Brookvale pool. She told me to look after the children because I was the eldest and she'd had enough. All day at school I'd be worrying and imagining what I'd be going home to.

All mom's life she would run away from things; if she didn't like the neighbours, she upped sticks and moved – she never stayed in one place long. Once she had got a house she exchanged it for another one: we had so many different houses when I was growing up that sometimes we forgot which house to go home to. I think mom would have made a good gypsy and been happy with a horse and caravan, and then if she didn't like a place she could just hitch up the horse and move on. She certainly had the wanderlust.

All this stress made us children hate our father even more for leaving us to such a fate, and mom's bitterness was rubbing off on us. She had poisoned our minds against our dad and it was dreadful living with mom in that frame of mind. When things went wrong, she took it out on us, having a wicked temper. We didn't dare answer back or not do as we were told, for she would get the broom and lamp out at us, saying she wasn't going to hurt her hands hitting us anymore. My sister and I had long hair and often had handfuls pulled out of our heads. Our John always had his head stuck in a book: he had the ability to cut himself off somehow and sit quietly reading, but he still got picked on for doing nothing. I used to say to him: "Watch out John, mom's on the warpath," and he'd make himself scarce. How we all grew up unscathed and did as well as we did I will never know, although we did grow up with an inferiority complex, thinking that we were not as good as others. We were timid, sensitive and easily hurt, but you learned to grow out of that. We all appreciated better lives later on and felt for others less fortunate. I hope we became more compassionate and generous to those in need, remembering how we had to go without. With all her faults, our poor mom would help any poor soul in need; she couldn't pass a tramp or a beggar without emptying her purse, telling them to go and have a cup of tea or something to eat.

In the park opposite where we lived, there was an old lady tramp who sat on the bench every day, and we used to watch her through the front-room window. She was there in all weathers. "Take this bottle of warm tea and this sandwich over to the woman, she must be cold and hungry," said my mom on many occasions, and I'd go over and give them to her. She never spoke, not even to say thank you. I don't know where she came from or where she slept at night – all I know is we felt responsible for her welfare.

Mom taught us that what you give away comes back to you a hundred-fold, and just think – that poor person could be Our Lord in disguise. So what you do for others you do for Him, but most of all she taught us to always appreciate what you have yourself.

When I was 13 years old, I fell on the ice in the school playground and banged my head, resulting in a huge bump on my forehead just like a large egg. After playtime I went back into class, but my vision was affected. I was seeing stars and flashing zigzag lights. I must have had concussion because the teacher said, "You will have to go to hospital," and asked if there was anyone willing to go with me. One girl put her hand up; she was one of the rich girls who I had always envied, because she was always dressed so smartly with lots of new clothes and her parents were rich. She had taken me home with her one day after school: her mother was Italian and her home was like a church, with lots of statues and holy pictures all over the house. At the hospital, I was put in a room to be examined. The doctor looked at my head but also told me to undress, as he wanted to examine my stomach – don't ask me why, perhaps it was for shock. Well, I got undressed down to my vest and knickers, and wanted the floor to swallow me up because of the state of my underwear. Before I left for school that day, the elastic had broken in my navy blue knickers and – not having time to mend it – mom gave me an enormous safety pin to put in them to keep them up. And there it was, for all to see. The nurse took the safety pin out and gave it back to me when I got dressed, all in front of my rich school friend.

Another embarrassing moment down to our mom was when she took us to the 'Onion Fair', and in case we got lost, or separated, she got a long piece of old rope and tied us all together. She said gypsies would steal children, and gypsies ran the fair. Sometimes, so we would be good, she threatened to sell us to the gypsies if we didn't behave. "Especially you, Patty, if you don't stop answering me back," she'd say, because I would say I didn't believe her when she said things like that. I was always getting into trouble for having a mind of my own. I remember someone gave us an old piano that badly needed tuning, but I learned to play by ear, I could play *Beautiful Dreamer* and *Chopsticks* and all the Christmas carols. I wish that I could have followed that up and had lessons.

When I was 14 years old my mom got special dispensation from the Church to marry again, this time in church as when she married dad it had been in a Registry Office. Mom met and married another Irishman, this time a good one. Patrick was his name. Our sister Moira was born and I became a second mother to her while helping mom to look after her. Mom would bathe and feed her, dress her and put her in the pram with orders for me to take her around the park for a few hours. She often kept me off school to help in this way; I didn't like school much, maybe because I'd lost so much time and couldn't catch up with the work.

Mom managed to get a council house again in Dulwich Road Kingstanding, because we were overcrowded at nan's, all sleeping in the same room, so once again we had our own house. I was glad to have my own bedroom again sharing with Carole as I had started my periods. At night, so that mom could go out, we all got a mug of hot milk with whisky in it to make us sleep. Many years later when I had children of my own and one of them wouldn't sleep at night, mom said: "Do what I did, put some whisky in her bottle."

"No way," I said. I can remember the room going round and round while I lay in bed at night and the cherries on the wallpaper doing a dance. She was amazed and said: "Fancy you remembering that." I remember a lot of things that mom did wrong, and I vowed never to do that when I grew up. I learned by her mistakes. She went on to say: "Well it never hurt you lot."

"How do you know, mom? I think it did." (Maybe she had pickled my thyroid, which I suffered with later on).

Working Girl

When I was 15 years old I left school and started work two days later in a sweet shop as a shop assistant, but I wasn't there long before I applied for a sales assistant job in Littlewoods chain store in Hawthorn Road, Kingstanding. When I started work, my wages were £2-10 shillings a week. Mom had the two pounds, and I had the 10 shillings.

With that I had to buy my own stockings and make-up, but I didn't have to pay for bus fares because my stepfather had bought me a bike, so I rode to and from work. He got it on the 'weekly', paying two shillings and sixpence a week for a couple of years. I'd never had a bike before – it was my pride and joy.

Around this time I had a friend with whom I worked at Littlewoods. One day we both went to the park and took out a rowing boat: it was our half-day and we were having a lovely time rowing around the pool. Then we did a very silly thing in changing over seats in the boat, so that she could try her hand at rowing. The boat capsized and we both ended up in deep water. Neither of us could swim. We would have drowned if it hadn't been for a young man who was watching us from the bank. He dived in to save us. He grabbed me first and managed to drag me to the bank, but my poor friend was going under for the third time. Park-keepers arrived on bikes blowing their whistles when they saw what had happened. The young man who had saved me went back in to save my friend, and thank God she was all right – just shaking, and minus her shoes, which she had lost in the water. Someone brought a blanket and a pair of slippers for her to walk home in. We did look like two drowned rats. Our Guardian Angels were with us that day, as we could have drowned. Thank

God for that young man. I never did find out who he was to thank him.

On the following day my friend didn't turn up for work, but her mother was in the shop, talking to the manager and telling him that she didn't want her daughter associating with that Pat Murray again, because I had nearly got her drowned. She left the job soon afterwards. I was shaken up too, but I couldn't stay off work as mom needed the money. Even when I had a carbuncle on my face, and in pain, I went to work but was told to go home. "You can't serve customers looking like that," the manager had told me.

A year later when I was 16 years old, it was at work in that shop that I met my future husband, Roy. He was 17, and was a cash-register mechanic who had come to service the tills. He came with an older man named Basil. Basil decided to do a spot of matchmaking. He came up to me and, standing by my counter, said: "You see that young man over there?" pointing to Roy. "Well, he's just told me that he fancies you, and wonders if you would like to go on a date with him." Then he went over to Roy and said, "That young lady over there has just said that she'd like a date with you." Neither of us had said anything of the sort, of course, but this was the start of our romance. We went to the pictures that night and after courting for two years we got engaged on my 18th birthday. On the same day, my grandfather passed away. It was the first death in the family I had experienced.

Roy

Roy and I started saving to get married. I was promoted at work to supervisor with a pay rise, so every week I would give something to Roy to put away. When we had saved about £30 he bought an old 1936 Morris 8 car, so that he could take me out more on trips and for picnics, and also when we went dancing we wouldn't have to wait for buses any more. We loved dancing, I had mixed feelings about him buying the car because we hadn't discussed it: we were supposed to be saving to get married and half the money was mine. But I forgave him because I was madly in love with him. He made me feel so good, and I can't remember a happier time in my life.

He wasn't a Catholic, but he used to come to Mass with me. Every Sunday I went to tea at his mom and dad's, and after tea we all played cards together. I started bringing little prizes for the winner, either toiletries or a box of chocolates. We all enjoyed our whist games very much.

About this time my mom and stepfather had applied to emigrate to Australia on the £10 assisted passage scheme. All our names had been put forward, but not Roy's, as they had done it before we got engaged. We all had to go for medicals and vaccinations against smallpox and cholera, and were all vetted by the authorities. Checking to see if any of us had ever been in trouble with the police, mom said that, "Australia only takes the cream from England." (Us the cream!)

I said: "And what about all the convicts that went over all those years ago, mom?"

We all passed our medicals except my stepfather. He had a hernia and was told to have the operation before going over, as the medical bills were steep in Australia and they didn't have a National Health system. It was like in America where you have to take out medical insurance for at least twelve months before making a claim or pay hefty medical bills. So he had the operation on the National Health. I had put the whole idea of going to Australia at the back of my mind, thinking it would never happen. Perhaps it was yet another of our mom's wild ideas to start a new life elsewhere. But the day came when we got our sailing papers, along with the date we were to set sail. It read: 'You will sail on Sunday 8th May 1960, from Tilbury Docks, at 2pm, on the P&O ship called the Orion.

Of course I was in turmoil because my fiancé wasn't included: how could I go to Australia and leave him behind? But then how could I let all my family go without me? If I stayed in England, I would be getting married and living with Roy's parents. I loved Roy but couldn't bear the thought of all my family being on the other side of the world without me. What had happened to 'the family that prays together, stays together'? We had all promised to stick together no matter what. What a dilemma. Roy and I decided to go to Australia House in London to ask if he could possibly come with us. It had taken over 18 months for my family to go through the procedure – how we thought that Roy could do it all in one day, I don't know.

This was on the Wednesday of the week the family was due to sail. We had an interview and explained our predicament, asking if there was any way that he could come with us. Needless to say, I was saying the rosary all the time. They asked if Roy was fit and healthy and gave him a medical there and then. Then they asked if he had a passport, which he hadn't.

"Not to worry," they said. "We can give you a travel document but you'll have to get your photo taken," which they arranged. "Regarding your vaccinations, you will have to have them done by the ship's doctor while you're on board."

"Does that mean he can go then?" I asked.

"Yes," they replied. Everyone was amazed with the outcome, but I knew that I had a powerful friend up there who had helped.

Roy went back to break the news to his parents and to resign from his job. It was a huge decision to make at just 20 years old, and he dearly loved his family, but everyone agreed it was a wonderful opportunity to see the world and have a new life. It all happened so quickly that his parents didn't have much time to object. They knew that Roy loved me, and despite the initial shock of losing their youngest son (the only one left at home), they didn't stand in his way.

We promised to come back in two years' time: we would regard it as a working holiday, then return home. The deal with the Australian government was that you stayed over there for at least two years; otherwise you would have to pay back the outgoing fare as well as the homeward fare. You went for just £10, subsidised by the government, but if you had to pay your own fares, it would have cost hundreds of pounds each.

Roy's mom and dad knew that my family and I would look after Roy. We didn't have much money but we sold the Morris and my bike, and with the little savings we had, we set sail for our new life 'Down Under'.

Sunday 8th May dawned and we travelled to Tilbury Docks to embark on the Orion. I was in awe as to how such a big ship could float on the water with all those people aboard and with such a huge amount of luggage. Before our ship could set sail, we had to wait until the Royal Yacht Britannia pulled out of the same harbour with Princess Margaret and Lord Snowdon aboard on their honeymoon. The eight of us were seen off by Roy's mother and father, my grandmother and her sister – great-aunt Winnie – who was sipping a bottle of whisky and crying. She seemed upset to see mom leaving, which I thought was rather strange because we had never had much to do with her and mom had never talked much about her. But as we were getting on board, she hugged mom saying: "I'll never see you again; I won't live much longer. Goodbye, love." I thought, well she's in her 70s and maybe we won't see her or her sister again either. "But we will be back in two years," I said.

Aunt Winnie died in the first couple of years. We got a letter from my nan telling us about it.

I felt mom couldn't wait to get on that ship and see the back of England and everything she was always running away from. But nothing made her happy, and from the minute we arrived in Australia she was finding fault with the place. We found it a beautiful place, another world: we thought we had died and gone to heaven. When we arrived on 10th June 1960, the weather was lovely and warm even though it was winter.

Australia

Everything grew bigger Down Under. The flowers, and fruit and vegetables were huge, the people warm and friendly too. 'This is the life,' I thought.

Our sea voyage had taken five weeks. We all had nice cabins on 'B' deck, towards the top of the ship with portholes for windows. Poor Roy had been put down on 'F' deck, which was below sea level with no porthole, and he shared the cabin with five other men. He was on the top bunk and said the ceiling was about six inches above his nose in bed, consequently he didn't spend much time in there. He was on deck or in the ship's Lounge all day, every day.

We wrote letters each day to loved ones back home and posted them on board – the letters were then sent home from different ports when we docked. I wrote to my grandmother, and both Roy and I wrote to his parents every day. Roy's mother saved all our letters, which we found years later when we had to clear her house. We found them in a bedside cabinet and re-read them: they brought back many memories of episodes in our life that I had forgotten about, such as when we first arrived in Australia my mother writing a song and having it put to music. It was about England and how much she missed it. It was called *My Lovely World and You*, and it went like this:

I sailed away across the sea,
But how lonely life can be
Now I have lost my lovely world, and you.

The lovely rose has lost its crimson gown,
And autumn leaves are falling over town.

The sky has lost its shade of blue
And I have lost my lovely world, and you.

But some day soon the clouds will roll away
And spring will bring another lovely day.
When, like a miracle come true,
I'll wake to find my lovely world, and you.

She entered a talent contest on TV in Adelaide along with others who had composed songs and she sang it on the show. I remember the show was called the 'Blair Schwartz Show'. It was in the early '60s and Mom still had a good soprano voice and did really well. I went with her and was also on the show. I, along with other contestants, played a game of snakes and ladders. It was a quiz game where you answered questions, and each time you got the answers right you moved up the ladder. I can't remember what I won; it was just a bit of fun. The show wasn't live; it was being shown on TV the following week. We all sat round the television to watch it and Roy took a dozen photos with our flash camera, but all that showed up were 12 photographs of the television set with a blank screen. The person who developed the pictures must have thought we loved our telly a lot.

On our cruise to Australia we sailed through the Bay of Biscay into the Mediterranean, to Port Said. It was our first port of call. We were not allowed to get off the ship, but lots of Egyptian traders came alongside in their little boats so we could buy lots of lovely leather goods. From Port Said we sailed down the Suez Canal into the Red Sea, where we made our second stop, this time at Aden. From there we sailed across the Indian Ocean to Colombo in Ceylon, where we went ashore and did some shopping. We had a guide to take us around places of interest, including a Buddhist temple, where you had to leave your shoes outside. The young boy, our guide, was called Sabu, and he looked just like Sabu the film star who made a few films and was often seen on-screen riding on an elephant. It was over 100°F that day, and Sabu was walking barefoot on hot pavements. The soles of his feet must have been like leather, because it didn't seem to bother him.

We saw lots of old men, dressed in what looked like just a napkin, sitting cross-legged in the street begging. We had never been abroad before; the furthest I had ever travelled was to Torquay in Devon on holiday the previous year, my first holiday ever. It was good to see how the other half lived, and as they say, 'travel broadens the mind'. At Port Said, the Egyptian traders had all sorts of things, mainly leather goods such as handbags, slippers, wallets, watches and stuffed toy camels which were all so cheap. Mom bought a box of 50 cigars, and for the rest of the trip Roy and my stepfather were smoking their heads off. The Egyptians sent their wares up in baskets on ropes for you to look at and if you wanted to buy anything you sent the money back down in the baskets. I think some of the English people were being dishonest – taking the goods and running off without paying, judging by the ranting and raving going on down below. I think I bought a handbag that day.

Our next stop was Aden and we saw many wonderful sights en-route; flying fish, schools of dolphins swimming alongside the ship, keeping up with us for miles, and then there were the Pyramids ranged along the shore. We spent most of the daytime on deck or in the swimming pool, and at night we danced in the ballroom or played cards and games. There was lots of entertainment to pass the time, with different artists appearing each night in cabarets. At one of the ports of call, a magician came aboard named Gully-Gully, who was very good. Every other night we had to put our watches forward by one hour until we reached Fremantle, which was 10 hours ahead of England. The food on board was first-class; it was like being film stars on a luxury cruise – even your washing was done for you. Every day you would put your dirty washing into a net bag with your cabin number on and the next day it would be brought back to you clean. There were ironing rooms available if needed. The cabins were cleaned daily and the beds made, it really was a lovely holiday and did us all the power of good.

We all became suntanned and put on weight. Roy's hair became blonder with the sun and he looked so handsome. Our only regret was that we didn't have a camera with us. To fill the days, I asked for my sewing machine to be got out of the hold so that I could do some sewing with some material I'd bought ashore in Ceylon. I made a couple of skirts – one for myself and one for my little sister, Moira. When word got round that I could sew, I had a full-time job doing alterations for the crew. The young steward lads kept bringing me their white trousers to be tapered into drainpipes, as it was the Teddy-Boy era, and that was the fashion. I didn't mind because they were all such nice boys, one being the waiter on our dining table. One night, he was carrying boiling hot soup over to the table when the ship rolled and he ended up on the floor covered in soup. We heard he was in a bad way with blisters on his back where he had been scalded.

One lad, a passenger who had the opposite cabin to ours, was smitten with our Carole and drove us mad playing the record *Oh Carole*, over and over every day. We soon got fed up with that.

We reached Australian waters and just over four weeks into our journey, we arrived in Fremantle, Western Australia, where about 500 migrants were disembarking for their new lives in Perth. We still didn't know our destination. There were about 1,500 migrants on board altogether: some would be getting off at Melbourne, some in Adelaide, and the rest in Sydney. Melbourne was our next port of call and it was there that another few hundred got off. We were then told that our destination was Adelaide but we'd have to disembark at Melbourne, and travel the rest of the way by train to Port Adelaide, and then on to the Hostel by coach.

After a 14-hour journey, we arrived at the Finsbury Hostel, Pennington, South Australia, all very tired and hungry. We were ushered into the canteen for tea and biscuits, and told our evening meal would be later on; it would be self-service and you could have as many helpings as you liked, so we looked forward to that.

Our luggage had travelled with us and was put into our chalets; rows and rows of wooden huts lined the roads, just like Butlin's holiday camps back home. Roy had his own chalet with one bedroom, and we had a three-bedroom one opposite. There were beds and a table and chairs inside, together with an electric kettle and cups to make a cup of tea. We had to share the toilets on the block.

We played cards at night, as there wasn't much to do. We went for walks around the camp to get our bearings, and to talk to other migrants, finding out how they were finding life 'Down Under'. Some of them had been there for years and not moved but that wasn't for us: we decided to find work and a house of our own as soon as possible.

Within a couple of days Roy had an interview with the National Cash Register Company in Adelaide City and got a job with them. I wasn't long behind him finding a job in the office of a textile mill called Actills. We discovered that it was quite expensive to stay in the Hostel and that the best bet would be to find our own place. There were plenty of houses to let in Adelaide, so there was no need to stay long where we were.

We'd been staying at the hostel exactly one month before we found what we were looking for. We were out shopping one day when we saw an advertisement in a shop window for a house to let. We phoned the number, went to see the house, and by some miracle it was just what we wanted, with lots of bedrooms and fully furnished. It belonged to an elderly gentleman who had been in hospital for months and was now in a nursing home and would not be returning home. His daughter was letting the place. There was however, one condition if we wanted it: the old boy had stipulated that no pork meat could be cooked on the premises. Apparently he was Jewish, and if we decided to take it then we would have to abide by his wishes. We thought it was a small price to pay to get out of that hostel, even if we did love our bacon sandwiches. We would just have to eat them elsewhere.

The daughter only lived a few doors away and would call every week for the rent. One day she called round to tell us that her father had died and the pork ban was lifted if we wanted to do ourselves a bacon sandwich. We were very pleased because it's the same old story – when you can't have something, you want it all the more. One night we had actually succumbed to our longings and cooked some bacon, but then we had a job of getting rid of the smell all over the house, and we were worried that we would be found out if the daughter came round. The price of bacon was sky-high then because all bacon had to be imported: there were no pigs in Australia as the climate was too hot for them.

While living in that house we discovered that there were plenty of houses to let in Adelaide, and Roy and I decided that there was nothing stopping us from getting married sooner rather then later, and renting a house of our own.

My job at the cotton mill was to add up all the quantities of material coming in and going out, using fractions to add up the yardage. At school I used to wonder what good learning about fractions would ever be to me, but taking notice back then saw me in good stead. It was at the mill that I met and made friends with an English couple from Bristol, Marion and Don, who had two little girls. They would invite us to their home for BBQs. They loved Australia and never wanted to go back to England, but it was easier for them because they had no family back home. But we were homesick, and missing our family back in England, and it was pulling at our heartstrings. Roy came home from work every night with the same question, "Any post from back home?"

We lived near the sea, as Adelaide is built around the coast. The beaches were miles of white sand with large beautiful seashells and hardly anyone on the sands. We used to go there a lot. While sitting looking out to sea, Roy used to say, "Just think, England is the other side of that ocean. I wish I could swim that far." I felt so sorry for him; homesickness is an awful thing, no matter how nice a place is. When you're far from home, there is no place like home and where your roots are. I'd think to myself, who in their right mind would want to go back to the cold, damp climate back home, away from all this lovely sunshine where you can dry the washing in minutes, and you never need to wear a coat: But too much of a good thing is not good either. When the summer came the heat was unbearable, and we longed for rain or a breath of fresh air. We never had air conditioning in the house and loved to drive to the shopping precinct where the air was blowing cold. At night we sat outdoors because it was too uncomfortable inside, but then the mosquitoes would eat us alive.

While in Adelaide we met another English couple, Josie and Fred. Josie came from Stafford and Fred was from London. They had emigrated a year before us with three children, and ended up having 11 children, losing one at birth. We became very close friends with them. Every year Josie was pregnant and suffered each time with an allergic rash all over her body; it must have been murder in the hot weather. We were godparents to one of their children. In the early years of our friendship we would take them out in our Triumph Mayflower car on picnics. Fred played the harmonica and we'd all sing along on the way. Fred loved to go to the races and we had many wonderful times together – we'd also go to their house and play cards.

One vivid memory I have of Fred is him mending all the children's shoes on an old iron last, just like my grandfather used to do. After we returned to England we kept in touch through letters. Sadly, Fred passed away some years ago and his eldest son Richard came over to visit, staying with us for a while. Then Josie came with her daughter Mary and her two children, then came Gerard, one of her other sons with his girlfriend, Clare: they have since married and have six children.

More recently Josie and another daughter Clare came over for a second visit. During Josie's first visit she and I went to Lourdes together and she said that was the highlight of her trip. Josie is now in her eighties and has a pacemaker fitted, and I live in hope of visiting her in the not-too-distant future. We now keep in touch by phone as well as letters. Strangely enough we both joined the Legion of Mary around the same time, on different Continents.

The house in Adelaide we lived in had, like many others, a tin roof which held the heat, making it impossible to sleep at night. I could never understand why they had tin roofs in such a climate – maybe it was because it was much cheaper than tiles, but when it rained it really rained heavily, and the noise of it hitting the tin roof was like a war zone.

Roy and I went to the local Catholic Church to see the priest about getting married. The church was called 'Our Lady of Mount Carmel' in Pennington. The priest took one look at us and said: "No, you are both too young." I couldn't see the problem; we were 20 and 21 in a month's time. My Mom married my dad at 17; we'd been together for four years and engaged for two. He relented, thinking we were younger, and then spoke to us separately in his study asking us if either of us were being forced into marriage, or if I was pregnant. I assured him none of that was the case and we wanted to get married because we loved each other. We'd found a little house, and although we couldn't afford a big white wedding and only my family of six would be present on the day, as long as we were married in church, we would be happy.

The wedding was fixed for a month's time, August 20 1960. Father Nugent, the priest, tried to persuade us to wait a further three months until the new church was finished on the same site as the old one. It was still being built, and as soon as it was finished the old church was to be demolished: so we had the choice of opting to be the last couple to be married in the old church, or the first couple to be married in the new one.

He took us round the nearly completed new church and proudly showed off the beautiful mosaic picture at the back of the Altar, showing Our Lady giving the scapula to St Simon Stock. I had learned all about that at school – I was always eager to learn anything about Our Lady. An Italian stonemason had made this grand mosaic picture and donated his work to the church. It was made up of thousands of tiny pieces of tile and was beautiful, but we really didn't want to wait another three months so we opted for the old church.

We had got only a month in which to send for our baptism certificates and make all the arrangements. We obtained the house to move into on the day of the wedding, not before, and we were in separate bedrooms at mom's house until then. We didn't have a honeymoon but were happy to go straight back to work and set up home in our first house together.

The wedding was a low-key affair with just six guests. I wore a blue-flowered dress and cream coat and a picture hat with a posy of violets. After the ceremony it was back to mom's on the bus for a buffet tea. Naturally, I would have liked a white wedding. It is every girl's dream to wear a beautiful wedding dress, and have all her friends and relations in attendance, but circumstances being as they were, and all the potential guests back in England, 13,000 miles away, what was the point? The main thing was that we were married in church and we had each other. We took some photos and sent them home. Starting out was a new adventure and we were so happy.

Married Life

A few days after the wedding, Roy said he would like to become a Catholic, which really pleased me. We saw Father Nugent after Mass that Sunday about him having instruction in the faith. For six months I went with him to his meetings – he was received into the church six months after our wedding, receiving his first Holy Communion and Confirmation shortly afterwards, with my brother John as his sponsor. Roy had been brought up in the Church of England faith and used to go to Sunday school; he knew more about the Bible than I ever did. He is a good man who believes like me, that our lives are in God's hands and that we should have morals and try to be good.

It was easier to live a good life over there: there weren't the same temptations as back home, and the missionary priests used to give such inspiring sermons at Mass that you would come away determined to do better. The weeks and months rolled by and a year later, I was expecting my first baby. I'd had to leave my job at the cotton mill because I'd contracted dermatitis after handling some khaki material left over from the war. It was when I had been asked to help out on the shop-floor because they were short staffed, and we were quiet in the office.

I went to the doctor's in a terrible state, covered in sores. The doctor said: "Oh no, not another one." Most of the workforce from Actills had visited the doctor with the same complaint, and really we all could have claimed compensation but didn't. The itching drove me mad. My mom made things worse by bathing the sores with ammonia. I got over it but never went back to that job. Meanwhile I had some more news to write home about in my letters now that I was pregnant.

We'd saved some money but with no medical insurance, the hospital and doctor's fees for the birth amounting to over £200, would use up all our savings and it would be back to square one.

Australia is a beautiful country, and Adelaide is the prettiest place, with lots of parks and beautiful gardens around the city. It's called the Queen of the South and the City of Churches because on every corner there seems to be a church. Some called it the 'retired state' as many elderly people retire there. We used to marvel at how fit the old people were – they could run for a bus with ease, and didn't seem to be riddled with arthritis, or stiff like the people back home. We then discovered that sometimes they weren't as old as we thought – it was just that the hot climate had made them more wrinkled.

We met and made friends with a Dutch couple, Rita and Ken. Ken told us that he worked on the oilrigs for an American company who were drilling in Adelaide at the time but would be moving in a few months all over the country. They only stayed in one place for around three months, and if no oil was found, they'd move on. They were going north to Mount Gambia next and were looking for men to go with them. Ken said the money was fantastic, about ten times what Roy was earning at the time, so Roy got a job with Reading and Bates, travelling around the country as a roughneck on the oil-rigs.

After a few months no oil was found in Adelaide, so they were moving on to a place called Port MacDonnell, about 300 miles away. I was near to having the baby and didn't want to have it in such a remote place, so we decided to compromise and have the baby in Adelaide, then join them in a couple of months' time. They kept the job open for him: good men were hard to find, as it was hard work in dangerous conditions.

Many workers on the rigs had died in accidents and that's why they were always looking for new men, but Roy was young and strong, and it was a marvellous opportunity for us to save our fares home, and maybe even have enough to put down on a house one day.

So six weeks after our son, Mark, was born we set off on the long journey to Port MacDonnell, in our old Triumph Mayflower, which was likely to break down at any time in the remote regions, without a house or people for miles and miles. One 60-mile stretch called the Birdsville Track was notorious for people getting stranded in and dying of thirst during the summer months. This was wintertime, but we were advised to take plenty of water with us all the same. We had to travel about 380 miles with a young baby, stopping every couple of hours for me to breast-feed him.

About 50 miles out of Adelaide we had our first puncture. Roy managed to fix that and when we got to Murray Bridge, we had the puncture repaired and continued on our way. We did have another flat tyre and changed that for the spare, so had to travel the last hundred miles without a spare. Our Hail Mary's were being said in earnest from then on, as our water supplies were running low too. When I think of the risks we took, I realise now that we were either very brave or very stupid, but it was a journey in faith, not knowing what we were going to find when we got there. Ken had promised to find us somewhere to live, but nothing could have prepared us for what was in store.

We had set out very early in the morning but didn't arrive at our destination (a little fishing village), until 10:30 at night. Ken and Rita were nowhere to be found. Seeing some lights on in a village hall, we made our way there to see if anyone knew where the oil riggers lived. There was a wedding reception going on, and the whole village had been invited, including Ken and Rita – so we found them and Ken took us to our house. I say house, but it was more like a broken-down old shack which had clearly not been used for years.

The whole house was dirty and dusty, with cobwebs and cockroaches running everywhere; there were a few sticks of furniture inside, including an old iron bed with a horsehair mattress. We were so exhausted after our long journey and so glad to have a roof over our heads that we would have slept on the floor. After making the bed with clean sheets we had brought with us, and with Mark asleep in his carrycot, we went to sleep.

The next day while Roy went to sign on for work, I set about cleaning the house and unpacking our belongings. I found there was no running water in the house, just a well down the garden. In the kitchen was a wood stove to heat the water and cook on, but before I could use the stove to boil a kettle, I had to chop wood to light it. The rent was just two pounds per week, with a bag of logs thrown in, which the owner brought each week when he collected the rent. We decided to make the best of it until we could find something better. There were lots of empty houses to rent in the village, many of them holiday homes only used during the summer, but if no oil was found on the drilling site, we would be out of there before then.

It was very lonely there. The men worked 12-hour shifts, and some nights I was on my own with a small baby. I knew only Ken's wife, Rita, and was pleased to have a friend, but she was more pleased to have me as a friend: she was near to having her first baby, which was due any day now and was eager to know what it was like to have a baby. I was so glad that I waited to have my baby in Adelaide before coming to such a remote place with no doctor or hospital for miles'. In fact, the nearest hospital was about 20 miles away. Once a month, a doctor came to the village with his travelling clinic, where you could go if you had any medical problems, but thank God we all kept healthy. I had brought a Dr Spock baby book, which my mother had given me, and I read that every day. I'd sit on the porch for hours reading or knitting to pass the time. There was only one store – it sold pretty much everything, but if they didn't have what I wanted, like baby wool, there was one bus a day to take me to another town. Sometimes I took myself off to do a bit of shopping where there was more variety to choose from and Rita used to come with me.

I thought to myself, 'what if Rita went into labour while the men were out at work? I would be no good at midwifery'. There were no mobile phones in those days, and no way of contacting Roy or Ken in an emergency. Sure enough one morning, at six o'clock, Rita was banging on my door; her waters had broken and she was in strong labour. I didn't know what to do – both men were out at work and not due back for hours.

I ran to the phone box outside the store to phone her doctor who said, "Get her to the hospital straight away." But I didn't drive, let alone have a car, so in desperation I knocked up the Old Italian couple that owned the store and told them that Rita was having her baby in my house. The man got in his delivery truck and drove round to pick Rita up and take her the 20 miles to hospital. I stayed behind with my baby to let Ken know what had happened when he got home from work.

I felt so sorry for her, as I watched the Italian man drive off in that old boneshaker-of-a-truck, with poor Rita, just 17 years old, and very frightened. If the shaking of that truck along the dirt roads didn't hurry up the birth, nothing would. 'She'll probably have that baby on the way', I thought to myself. As it happened she got there in time; she had a little boy that day.

Roy and Ken arrived home after their nightshift, tired and dirty. When I told Ken what had happened, and that Rita was at the hospital, he wasn't concerned. He said, "She'll be all right. I'm shattered, I'm going to bed and will see her tonight". When I think of the panic-stations earlier that day, with me imagining that I'd have to deliver his baby, and the sight of his wife crying for him, his lack of concern baffled me.

A few days later Rita and the baby were home and we did everything together. I showed her how to make chocolate cake and she taught me how to make goulash and some Dutch dishes. She also showed me how they knit in Holland, back-to-front to how we did it. She never had to turn the knitting pins around when she came to the end of the row – she'd just go back the same way, like doing it left-handed. She didn't speak much English, and often got mixed up with her words and made me laugh. Ken was teaching her all the wrong words too.

One day we caught the bus and went into the next town to do some shopping. While we were in a big department store we needed to find the toilet. Rita went over to the assistant to ask where they were and it all came out wrong. I couldn't repeat what she said, but I apologised to the woman explaining that my friend didn't know much English.

It wasn't long before Roy and I found another house to rent in the fishing village. It was a nice big house, with running water and all mod-cons; no more getting up at the crack of dawn to chop wood and get the fire alight in the stove, and no more fetching water from the well before we could have a cup of tea. Our new home was a large, log cabin, like those in American films, like *Bonanza*, with a huge fireplace big enough to burn half tree-trunks on. There were plenty of woods nearby, so we'd have no trouble finding firewood.

I loved it there; it was fully furnished and in lovely surroundings with a sea view. I was relieved to find it nice and clean, not like the previous place where, when I pulled down the dusty curtains to wash them, a huge, hairy, tarantula spider crawled out across the wall. I was horrified to think that that monster had been hiding behind there all the time we were sleeping a few inches away. What if it was poisonous? What if it had bitten the baby? I did no more than grab Mark and run over to Rita's to tell her what had happened. Ken happened to be home that day as he was on a different shift to Roy. I said I was afraid to go back in that house. Imagine if there were more of those big hairy monsters like that in there, I'd never seen anything like it. Rita sent Ken back with me to deal with it. The size of it even gave him a start; it hadn't moved from where I left it. After a few choice swearwords, Ken squashed it with his foot on the wall. I'm not exaggerating when I say that his size 11 shoes did not cover it. Things grow bigger Down Under. It was huge, and the most frightening thing I've ever seen.

Later on I was assured by one of the village fishermen that the spider wasn't poisonous, and that it would have been a 'lazy huntsman' spider, which look more frightening than they really are; they get a lot of them in that part of the country. From then on, I was wary of spiders and snakes (there were some scary moments with them too).

Once, when I was crossing a field of long grass, with Mark in my arms, I nearly stepped on a snake. He was curled up with his head sticking up, just looking at me as if to pounce. I never ran so fast in all my life, and never took the short-cut across that field again. Another time, Roy was clearing an overgrown back garden, which was like a jungle. Underneath the weeds were corrugated iron sheets on the ground. When he lifted these up to dispose of them, he found millions of Red Backs; tiny spiders that are poisonous. One bite from them can cause serious illness. They scattered everywhere, even over his shoes and up his trousers, there he was stripping off all his clothes brushing himself down, but fortunately he wasn't bitten. Roy did no more than get a can of petrol and burn the whole patch where the spiders were. In our new home in Port McDonnell, I spent many hours sitting on the porch knitting, but missing the family. I thought it would be nice to invite them to come for a little holiday and stay with us. We had plenty of room, and it would be a nice break for them by the sea.

Visitors

*M*om and Moira came first for a week and we met them at the railway station. When it came time for them to go home, our car broke down on the way to the station on a quiet country lane early in the morning. There was a thick mist that covered the car; it was quite eerie. We couldn't fix the car in time to get them to their train and mom was really worried that they were going to miss it. An old truck with two hillbillies was coming towards us and Roy flagged them down. Mom said, no way was she getting in with two unsavoury characters like them! But we didn't have any choice if she wanted to get to the station in time, and we didn't know how long it would be before another car would pass. "What are you trying to do to us?" mom said. You hear of such things happening in remote regions like this, but in they got and I prayed they'd be all right.

Mom later told us that the two strange men never spoke a word all the way into town. She and Moira were terrified but they got their train in time and were relieved to get back home safely. We can laugh about it now, but our mom never let us live that episode down, swearing that Roy was trying to get rid of her.

The following week we got a letter at the post office from my brother John, who was now in the Police Force. He'd just passed out from being a cadet and was now a proper law-enforcer. The day John passed out as a Police Officer it was a boiling hot day, 110 degrees in the shade, and many of the men in full uniform were literally passing out with the heat. They were falling down like flies on the parade ground – passing out in more ways than one! John had some leave coming up and asked if he and a friend, also named

John, could come for a week or two for a holiday with us. I was over the moon because it was very lonely up there and it would be great to have some more company again.

It was lovely to have them with us. They took us out for picnics and for rabbit-shooting in the forest. We caught a couple of bunnies and made a rabbit stew, which was delicious; it reminded me of nan's rabbit stews as a child. We saw kangaroos in the woods, and driving through one day we came across a dead baby kangaroo lying in the middle of the road. It must have been run over, but some time ago, because it was as stiff as a board. John's mate was a bit of a joker and he stood it up in the middle of the road, put one of Mark's nappies on it, then an old hat on its head and a cigarette in its mouth and said: "Just imagine what the next driver along this road will think when they come across that." We left there in a fit of giggles; I know it wasn't nice but we did laugh.

One night the two Johns decided to try their hand at fishing off the jetty. They told me not to wait up, as they didn't know how long they would be, so with Roy on nightshift at work, I went to bed. About four in the morning I heard a noise outside and went to let them in. There were the men with a big sack full of fish, but what I saw inside the sack was absolutely fascinating. It looked like a mass of dark-blue flapping objects, covered in coloured sequins glistening in the dark. Purple, pink, green and turquoise; I'd never seen anything like it before. In fact they were crayfish (small lobsters) – 106 of them.

"What are we supposed to do with this lot, John?" I asked.

"Cook them," he said. "But in the meantime, we'll have to fill the bath up with cold water and put them in." Well they were all flapping about in the water, making such a noise. We went to bed but were woken up about 7am with a loud shout.

"What the heck is going on here?" It was Roy, home from

work, filthy dirty and wanting a bath, only to find it full of lobsters.

That day we found some house bricks to make a temporary barbeque in the back garden, made a fire and put a bucket of water on to boil to cook them in. We found the best way to cook crayfish was to drop them into the boiling water, which seemed cruel because they squeal when you put them in. When they turn bright red, they are cooked; it just had to be done. By the end of the day we had cooked all 106 of them. We kept most of them in the freezer but we were eating fish for weeks after that, and the whole house stank of fish. After having our fill of the lovely white meat, we had so much left over that we decided to give some away. The villagers were all fishermen and probably had enough of their own catch, but there was a convent nearby, and wondering if the nuns would like some, we took a big box over to them. They were most grateful.

We got to know the nuns at Mass on Sundays, once a fortnight; we only had Mass every other week in the village but on alternate Sundays there was Mass in another town a few miles away. One of the nuns asked us if we had room in our car for some of the Sisters to have a lift to Mass, as they didn't have enough transport for all of them, so we were happy to oblige.

The first time we took three of the Sisters, our car seats were dusty and dirty from Roy's job; I had meant to clean them beforehand. When they got out of the car, their black habits were covered in dust. I was mortified, knowing how particularly clean nuns are, but they made light of the situation, dusted themselves down and laughed about it. These young girls were so joyful, singing hymns all the way home in the car. I wondered if I had become a nun would I have been like that, but decided, 'No, I'm not cut out for that life, shut up in a convent with all those rules'. I loved life on the outside and was very happy as a wife and mother.

One of them held the baby for me to get out of the car and looked down on him so lovingly, I wondered if she regretted never knowing the joy of motherhood, because nuns don't get married or have children, they are married to Christ; it's a calling. They all seemed very happy in their vocation and I was happy in mine. But I made sure that the seats were clean in future.

While the two Johns were with us, we went on trips together. We had heard of the Blue Lake of Mount Gambia, a tourist attraction, and decided to take a look. After parking the car we went over to the barrier and looked down into a big ravine where there was an oval lake of milky blue water. It was supposed to be so deep that it was bottomless, and the milky colour of the water was caused by the white stone round the perimeter. It was a beautiful natural site, one that could only have been created by God. At night, the stars are so big; millions lit up the sky, shining so brightly you felt that you could reach up and pluck one out of the sky. They looked so near, which reminded me of the words of the hymn:

Oh Lord my God, when I, in awesome wonder
Consider all the worlds thy hands have made.
I see the stars; I hear the rolling thunder,
Thy power throughout the universe displayed.
Then sings my soul, my Saviour God to Thee
How great Thou art
How great Thou art.

Another thing I remember was that there was no twilight, like back home – instead, one minute it was light and the next it was dark; it seemed to come on quicker there.

At night, when sitting outdoors, being too hot to stay inside we were bitten alive by mosquitoes, and believe me, too much of a good thing such as hot sunny weather, isn't good for you. The long hot summers used to get everyone down. We longed for rain and a breath of cold air was life itself; we are never satisfied. I remember asking an elderly lady how she had put up with the heat all her life and she said, "It was nothing compared to when I was a girl. We used to hang wet sheets and blankets up the walls inside the houses to cool the rooms down." She went on to say: "We wouldn't have all the lovely fruit and plants without the hot sun."

In lots of ways, Australia was behind the times compared to England; the fashion in clothes was not so up-to-date: the clothes were lighter and more suitable for the climate but in old-fashioned styles, like my mother used to wear when I was a child. I guess it's all changed now, but in the early sixties it was more like in the '30s and '40s.

It was a multi-cultural nation with every nationality, but in the 1960s the only black people there were the Aboriginals. I remember the famous pianist Winifred Atwell was on tour in Australia and wanted to stay there, but was refused entry and had to return to England. Later, some black people were allowed to stay in the country but for no longer than two years. That has all changed now too. Some of the Aborigines lived in the cities but most lived in the bush then.

Working On the Oilrigs

After about a year working on the oilrigs as a 'roughneck', Roy came home one night saying that there had been a terrible accident at work: the steel rig had collapsed, falling down on top of the men working below. He was lucky to escape with his life, as he had managed to jump clear just in time. For months after that he would jump in his sleep, having nightmares reliving the scene.

I was so thankful that he wasn't killed that night, and although we had hoped to stay a while longer and save more, it just wasn't worth it, travelling around with a young child. So when the drilling period in that particular town came to an end, we decided to pack up and return to Adelaide – especially as the next drilling site was to be in Darwin, one of the hottest places up north. We heard from Rita and Ken that it was a desolate place up there, with leper colonies in the place they went to; the oil riggers used to donate food and clothing to the poor lepers leaving them outside the gates.

We stayed with mom, as she still had the large house near the city, while we looked for somewhere to live. We found a bungalow that was divided into two flats, and we rented one, which consisted of a bedroom, lounge, kitchen and bathroom with a hallway dividing the separate dwellings. The other side was let to a German couple who didn't stay long: people in Australia move around a lot. When they left, the owner said she was putting the bungalow up for sale. We liked it: we had some money saved and saw it as an investment if we bought it, as well as an opportunity to make more money by doing it up and selling it on at a profit later. We asked the owner if she would sell it to us and she agreed. So now we were buying our own house at 34, Arlington Terrace, Welland, South Australia.

Buying Our Own House

*A*round this time, I discovered that I was expecting my second child – again, with no medical insurance. Whatever money we had left would be swallowed up in maternity fees, but we lived in hope of being able to sell the bungalow later on after doing it up, enabling us to go home, this time with two children.

I was expecting this baby around Christmas and dreaded being heavily pregnant in the height of the summer. Sure enough, it was murder. We didn't have any proper air-cooling system in the house, only a couple of fans. My sister, Carole, was pregnant with her first baby, having married Bruno, a German boy, the year before. He was a bricklayer by trade and earned good money, and was very good to her. Her baby was due around the same time as mine; we still talk about the time we were both nine months pregnant in 110° F, walking down the street together like two fat ladies waddling, wiping the perspiration from our brows and necks. The well at the front of my neck was always filling up with water and the constant wiping made it sore. I couldn't stand the heat; it was a real penance and I wanted to return to a cooler climate.

The bungalow was a lovely house, with a huge back garden, at the bottom of which were 12 almond trees and a large apricot tree. With so much fruit we could never eat it all, so we sold some to the local fruit shop. We also collected bucketfuls of almonds and shelled them, which was easy, as they were paper shells, and then sold them to the nut stall in the market. We had a fig tree, an orange tree and a lemon tree and we used the land to grow every vegetable you could name, even a vegetable that we had never tasted in England, called a trombone. I guess it is what's known now as butternut squash. We were amazed at how quickly everything grew and how big everything was, as long as you watered the plants day and night. Our melons and cucumbers were so big they could have won a prize. Along the length of the house at the back, we had a grapevine with so many grapes I was forever sweeping rotten grapes up off the floor, as it smelled like a brewery. It was the same with the rotten apricots that had fallen off the tree.

You would think with all the fresh fruit and vegetables we ate that we'd be healthy, but not me. Every day I'd be in and out of the shower all day, and by teatime I'd be sitting in a bath of cold water with my swimming costume on, to cool down. What I didn't know at the time was that I had an overactive thyroid, and the hot weather was very hazardous to the complaint; unfortunately it wasn't diagnosed until years later

It was while collecting apricots off the tree in our garden that I went into labour; as I was reaching up high, I felt the first twinges, which then developed into stronger pains by night time.

Mark was poorly at the time and I didn't want to leave him, so I delayed going into hospital as long as I could; it was very worrying watching him so poorly in his cot. He was only 20 months old, just wearing a nappy because of the heat, I could see his little heart beating in his chest trying to breathe with his asthma. On top of that, he also had the measles. I was reluctant to leave him but eventually I had to go, leaving Roy to cope.

It was 115° F in the shade that day and I was glad to be in an air-conditioned hospital. I got there just in time before the baby shot out like a bullet from a gun; I had been scheduled to have a Caesarean section with this birth, as I had pre-eclampsia (toxaemia) in pregnancy and was told that there would be a danger of losing either one of us during the birth if I didn't have a Caesarean. As it happened, there was no time to prepare me for theatre. My second son was born too quickly: he was a blue baby and was in trouble, and wouldn't breathe. For a while it was pretty worrying and I was saying my prayers in earnest again. I had left home praying for our first son to recover and was now praying that I wouldn't lose this one: "Please Lord, don't let him die."

Seeing my baby in danger, I asked the hospital staff to run next door to the Catholic Church and fetch a priest to come and baptise him. Within a couple of minutes the priest was there and said. "Quick Mrs Brookes, what name have you chosen for the baby?" I hadn't thought of any boy's names, as we were hoping for a girl this time, but the name David came into my head and I blurted it out and that was what he was baptised as. David pulled through, thank God, but had to stay in hospital for a month as he was underweight; five pounds was too tiny to go home, so I went home without him after 10 days, leaving him in the incubator. I had to 'express' my milk and take it up twice a day to the hospital for him.

He was a very thin and delicate baby, and I promised that once I got him home, I would soon fatten him up, which I did and he became such a bonny baby. The hospital fees for keeping him there for a month were very high, so bang went all our savings again.

Our Second Child

*H*omesickness is an awful thing: Roy missed his family back home so much. Those sayings, such as 'the grass is always greener on the other side of the fence' and 'there's no place like home' are true, even if you are in a much more beautiful place and have a better lifestyle. I knew my husband wasn't happy; I'd dragged him out there and we had promised to return in two years, but already three and a half years had gone by, and we were still there.

There were bushfires in the Adelaide Hills and sometimes we would watch them from mom's back garden, hoping they wouldn't reach the town. Fortunately they were always brought under control. These fires were almost always started by accident, by people on picnics in the hills; it only needed a careless match or a spark from a picnic fire that hadn't been doused properly, and it would spread so quickly, as everything was so dry.

One day, Roy and I almost started a bushfire of our own up there. We'd been in the Hills looking for opals, as we had been told that some had been found there; my brother later found some and had a large one put in a pendant to hang round the neck on a chain that he gave to me. We didn't find any but, on the way home in the car, Roy lit a cigarette, which he dropped when we came to a sharp bend in the road called the Devil's Elbow. (a well-known accident spot). The cigarette landed on some screwed-up paper from our picnic food and quickly set it alight. There was a lot of traffic on the road, so we couldn't just stop driving round sharp bends as other cars behind would crash into us, so there I was, frantically trying to put out the fire. I was fighting a losing battle, but eventually Roy was able to stop in a safe place, get some water out of the boot and put it out. What a fright we had; the people in passing cars were looking really worried too. I had visions of us being blown to Kingdom Come if the fire had reached the petrol tank. I think our Guardian Angels were alert that day.

When we went to the pictures, we used to go to a drive-in cinema, which is something we never had back home. You'd park your car in a huge field with a giant cinema screen; speakers were alongside on posts, and to hear the sound you had to insert your money. It was a novel way to see a movie, and much cooler.

We packed so much into our life in Australia, and it gave us so many memories to look back on; we can't say we haven't lived. We stayed in so many houses in 'Oz', like the time we came back from the oil-rigs and lived with mom for a while, looking for a house of our own. Roy was out of work and was offered a job in Melbourne, so we decided to take a trip there to 'suss it out'. Mom was fed up with where she was living, as usual (she never settled anywhere for long) and she said: "We will all come with you." They packed up, leaving everything, to go on another adventure. We went along with it, not thinking about where we would all live once we got there. My stepfather was out of work and Roy said maybe he could get him work too. We had a big estate car by now and we piled everything we could in it, cramming it full of suitcases and household stuff. There was mom, dad, Frank, Moira, Roy, and Mark in his carrycot, and me. Seven of us on another hare-brained adventure.

We did over 500 miles that day, getting to Melbourne only to find the job vacancy had been filled and there was no work available; we'd been misinformed. We took one look at Melbourne and didn't like it one bit. It was similar to London: everyone was dashing about and too busy to take the time of day to speak to us or help us to find somewhere to stay or work. Realising that it wasn't as we had hoped for, we decided to do an about-turn, and head back to Adelaide. Having burnt our bridges, now with nowhere to go, nowhere to live when we got there, we thought, 'what have we done?' We couldn't all descend on our Carole, and our John was living at the police barracks, so where would we go? What were we to do? When I think of the stupidity of it all, we must have been mad, but we trusted in God to see us all right.

We were all very tired after the long trip to Melbourne and Roy couldn't be expected to do any more driving that day, so we booked into a guest house for the night. We found a nice bed-and-breakfast place down a country lane and paid for two rooms on the ground floor, the men in one, and us women in the other. We had the window wide open all night and in the morning were woken up by a horse's head, sticking through the window, licking our faces. When we had arrived in the dark the night before, we didn't know there were horses in the back garden. It was a lovely guesthouse, away from the city and off the beaten track; we were lucky to have found it. The people who ran it were very nice. After breakfast we all piled into the car and set off on another long journey; we arrived in Adelaide at 10:30 at night – and homeless.

Mom suggested buying a newspaper and looking down the houses-to-let column; one thing about good old Adelaide was that there were always plenty of houses to let. There were two possible ones, both fully furnished: the first didn't answer the phone; but the second one did. "Yes, it is still to let," said the man, "and you can view it tomorrow." I explained that we had just got into town from Melbourne and had nowhere to stay and would it be possible to see it tonight? He seemed a bit put out; you can imagine how daft we must have seemed but agreed, and let it to us that very night.

Like a miracle, there were just enough beds in it for all of us. We paid the man a deposit and all fell into bed. So yet another fine mess we had got ourselves into; I couldn't do it now, but we were young and gullible and game for anything then.

Mom actually liked that house because it was in the city and near to all the shops, and she stayed on there long after we got our bungalow. We'd been in the bungalow a while before David came home from hospital and I soon fattened him up as I'd promised to do. Although he'd been baptised in hospital, he still had to go to church for the ceremony and that happened when he was just over a month old.

We still didn't have our fares back home, and a couple of years down the line we were expecting baby number three. I was upset about that because we would never get home now, not with more medical bills. Roy had got another job as a window fitter, and was earning decent money but it was only enough to live on and we couldn't save anything. We'd bought some furniture and had done the house up nicely and were comfortable where we were – but still had that yearning to go home.

I was at mom's one day, distraught, saying: "Why is it that every time we try to get home, something happens to stop us? It's been five and a half years now, and I can see us here for good. We are done for; I can't have another baby in this climate and don't know how I'll cope with three little ones under four." I couldn't understand why things have turned out like they had.

The answer she gave me has stuck in my mind ever since. She was dead right. She said, "Where's your faith love? God's never let us down yet. Maybe it's not the right time."

"What do you mean, mom?"

"Well, it's all in God's plan, our whole lives are mapped out for us, and the house you will live in the future is not ready yet. The people you will encounter on your path of life aren't there yet; those who will be part of your life haven't come together yet. Even your children's partners are not in the right place for them to meet. You'll see love, it will all fall into place and will fit together like a jigsaw puzzle."

Those words were real words of wisdom, and very true. I realise now that if I had come home to England sooner, we wouldn't be living in this house. I probably wouldn't have all these grandchildren, and I wouldn't have made all the wonderful friends, or joined the Legion of Mary. Yes it's all in God's plan, and He knows best.

My stepfather died shortly after this with lung cancer and mom decided to take Moira and herself back to England, leaving Frank with us. He was 17 and working as a bellboy in a hotel in town. Mom didn't have much money but we all helped out with the fares, and off she went home to look after my grandmother, who wasn't well. Mom made us a promise before she left, to somehow get us back too and she did. She went to visit Roy's parents who acted as guarantors on a loan, and four months later we set sail back to England.

We sold our bungalow to my sister, Carole and her husband, who had always liked our house, and Bruno, being a builder, had great plans for it, and could do a lot more to it.

They had two more children in that house and a few years after we left Australia, a supermarket was built backing onto their garden – they sold part of the land for a car park and were paid handsomely for it. If we had stayed a while longer, we would have had enough money to return to England and buy a house ourselves, but it wasn't to be. As it was we made just enough out of the sale of the house to pay back the loan and for our long trip back.

Journey Home

I had got on that ship at five months pregnant and was lucky to be aboard, as that was the latest stage of pregnancy you could be accepted on a ship on a long journey; the shipping company would not take responsibility if anything should happen. I wasn't showing when I started the voyage, but by the time we arrived home I was quite big. I remember falling down the stairs two weeks into the journey, when the ship rolled, and was worried in case I'd lose the baby. But everything was fine.

One of our ports of call was Port Said, Egypt, where Arabs came aboard selling their wares. One of them looked at me with two little boys, and pregnant again, and said to Roy, "Lucky man. Fertile wife. Plenty sons; you are very rich." Apparently, the more sons men have, the more fortunate they are considered. He then said to Roy, "How much you want for your wife?"

Roy looked at me and jokingly said, "How much do you reckon I'd get, love?"

Again the Arab persisted. "I give you my boat and everything on it," showing him gold chains and watches as examples.

"No way," chuckled Roy.

"OK, two boats. That one, and my brother's boat over there," he said, pointing to the boats down below. "And a camel."

We laughed it off, but over the years it's been a long-standing joke in our house; when we have a disagreement, Roy reminds me that he should have sold me to the Arabs long ago.

Once in rough seas, I think it was in the Bay of Biscay, I

was sitting in the ship's lounge with the children on my lap, saying my prayers because the boat was being tossed about and I was really scared we might sink. We were all seasick and I was trying to get the boys off to sleep by singing to them. The words of the hymn, *Hail Queen of Heaven*, came into my mind, so I was singing them to myself:

Hail Queen of Heaven, the ocean star,
Guide of the wanderer here below.
Thrown on life's surge we claim thy care,
Save us from peril and from woe.
Mother of Christ, Star of the sea,
Pray for the wanderer, pray for me.

And then another hymn: '*For Those in Peril on the Sea.*' They call it the cruel sea and it is true.

Our voyage home took longer than our outward journey, as it was a smaller ship, an Italian Sitmar Liner called *The Fairsea* a 24,000 ton ship whereas the Orion ship was 36,000 tons. All the crew were Italian, as was the food and not as nice as on the P&O ship. There was no entertainment aboard, and the only games for the children were sliding from one side of the ship's lounge to the other when it rolled. There was a fancy dress competition for the children and we wondered what we could dress them up as, but I had a brainwave. As we would be spending Christmas on board, we had packed a cowboy outfit for Mark – but what about David, aged two? I cut up one of Roy's white shirts, made a halo out of a piece of wire covered in silver paper and a wand out of a stick with a star, and he made a lovely angel. We still have the photo of them dressed up walking along the deck to be judged.

Our return journey took a different route to our outbound crossing, covering the eastern side of Australia and visiting Sydney, where we spent a day ashore. Sydney Harbour is situated in the heart of the city, where we went shopping. I bought two large tins of powdered milk because we discovered that there was no fresh milk aboard for the children. Then the ship went on to Brisbane, where most of the houses were built on stilts. After leaving Australian waters, we visited Singapore, which was a sultry place, with lots of flies and with sewage running down the gutters; I couldn't live there. As we walked along the streets, market stalls displayed strange-looking foods, which looked like dead beetles and insects. When we got to Naples, most of the crew got off to go home for Christmas; a skeleton crew stayed on until we reached Southampton.

We spent Christmas Eve in Naples, which was nothing like I'd imagined, because they say 'See Naples and Die'. I thought it would be beautiful. Well, maybe the city itself was, but we were near the docks, and it was bitterly cold – the first time we felt the cold air that we had so longed for in Australia.

We found a café open for a warm drink and some fresh milk for the children; they had missed that on the ship. We went to Midnight Mass in Naples, then spent Christmas Day aboard ship, without even a Christmas tree. We had the choice of disembarking at Naples and travelling the rest of the way by train, which is what a lot of the other passengers did, but we opted to stay on board until we reached Southampton. Big mistake. We hit very rough seas in the Bay of Biscay and were all sick as dogs, and also had upset tummies. Our cabin stank to high heaven, and by the time we got off the ship we were all quite ill. It was New Year's Eve when we caught the train to Birmingham, and New Year's Day 1966 when we arrived at Snow Hill Station. We were much the worse for wear from our travels, but grateful to be back home – at long last. In hindsight we should have disembarked at Naples, sparing ourselves that awful experience.

We were back in England at last, I was six and a half

months pregnant

Roy's mom and dad, and our old friends Pat and Brian, were there to meet us. I was worried about the children catching a cold, as the weather was freezing; I was glad that we had bought them both warm padded shell suits with fur-lined hoods in Singapore with our last bit of money. They looked like little Eskimos.

Back Home

We arrived in England with an Australian £10 note, which we couldn't cash at the station, so in fact all we had were two suitcases. We were penniless, and very glad to see the family.

We were back in England at last, after nearly six years, and I was six and a half months pregnant with my third baby.

Our Frank, who had travelled home with us, was dropped off at mom's house that she managed to find to rent, where she was looking after my grandmother who now lived with her at 74 Edwards Street, West Bromwich.

When I gave birth to our baby girl, Caroline, we were living at Roy's parent's home at: Coneyford Road, Shard End, Birmingham, and were there for twelve months.

Roy's mom and dad couldn't do enough for us, putting hot-water bottles in the beds to keep us warm, but it wasn't the best way to start the New Year, all feeling ill. You could say that we had travelled halfway around the world, but we didn't want to go travelling again. We had done our roaming and were now content to stay put and settle down.

On the ship, unbeknown to us at the time, Frank had been put in the same cabin as a young drug addict, who had been deported by the Australian authorities. I wasn't happy about Frank being with him: he was an unsavoury character who sat at our dining table with us, and seemed to have a chip on his shoulder. He was poorly dressed, and as the weather got colder, I felt sorry for him and gave him some of Roy's clothes, and thinking his feet must be cold in his old sandals and no socks, let him have a pair of Roy's shoes and socks to wear.

One evening at dinner, I happened to mention that Frank's brother was a sergeant in the police force in Adelaide, which infuriated him, and he muttered something like, 'well I hope he dies in the gutter." He hated the police who had deported him. When we had docked at Singapore, he took our Frank ashore and gave him some cannabis. I thought something was wrong when neither of them turned up to dinner, so I took them both some food down to their cabin. I just thought they were in a drunken state and were sleeping it off. We didn't learn about the drugs until after we had arrived back in England.

A few months after we arrived home, I got a phone call from mom saying that Frank was in trouble with the police – he had been found in a café in possession of drugs. That was the start of a long and difficult problem with Frank; he would steal from his mother and grandmother to feed his habit and was in and out of trouble, all due to drugs. He needed stronger and stronger drugs; these caused mental illness and eventually resulted in him taking his own life. I often wonder if he had stayed in Australia whether his life would have gone differently? He was only 18 years old when he came home: he was easily led and got into bad company.

My grandmother passed away a year after we arrived back home. I was glad that I was able to see her again before she died. She held her great-granddaughter, Caroline, a few times, and said she could now go in peace, after seeing us all again. It was a shock for me to lose my lovely nan, who I'd loved and written to every week for six years. She had suffered a stroke and I would sit with her in her bedroom. One day, she told me not to sit on the bedside chair because Our Lady was sitting there and I was standing on her gown. I wondered about that and believe that because she loved Our Lady so much, maybe She did come to take her to Heaven and was with her when she was dying. For six years I had prayed to Our Lady to be with my grandmother when she died and maybe She was answering my prayers. Who are we to say otherwise?

I mentioned this to a priest who called to see nan and he wasn't surprised. He said: "Well, perhaps God wanted her to see Our Lady and that is how it had to be." Mom thought that my grandmother was hallucinating with the drugs she was on, but I believed nan.

Nan asked mom for a priest just before she died, but mom thought she had said 'piece' and brought her a sandwich. Just before mom realised what she really wanted, a knock came on the front door; it was the local Catholic priest who was passing and was suddenly drawn to the house. He stood at the door saying: "Something tells me I'm needed here," and he was. Wasn't that strange? Nan died soon after.

Mom was now on her own with Moira and Frank. One day she went to town, leaving Frank at home and when she got back the house was stripped bare. Frank had called a furniture dealer in and sold the lot for money to buy drugs. Mom called the police and they found all her stuff in the second-hand furniture shop up the road and got it back for her. Frank became more and more disorientated and was in and out of hospital. On one occasion, a doctor told us Frank had taken LSD, which is like acid to the brain, and he had done irreparable damage to his mental state. He became depressed and suicidal and tried many times to take his own life. We were still living with the in-laws, and couldn't help much, with three young children. I worried about what all this was doing to mom; all this stress was taking its toll on her and she developed angina.

Twelve months after we got home I found a house to rent. We had applied to Birmingham Council for somewhere to live but were told that there was a long waiting list: it would be many years before they could help us because we weren't overcrowded where we were. It was a three bed-roomed house and we had two of the bedrooms, with Roy and I and the baby in one, and the boys in the other, so our only hope of a home of our own was to find a privately rented one. I walked the streets every day looking for a place to live while Roy was at work. I set out every morning with the three children – Caroline in the pram, David sitting on the end of the pram and Mark toddling alongside – but it seemed no one wanted to rent to people with three young children; they preferred business couples.

It wasn't long before I began to wonder what we'd come to and what we'd done We should have stayed in Australia, in our nice bungalow where I could dry the washing and baby's nappies in minutes in the hot weather, whereas over here it had rained every day for months. The dark days were so depressing.

Christmas came and went, and in January, with snow on the ground I was still trudging the streets, looking for somewhere to live. I was willing to take anything, as long as it was our own, because as good as Roy's parents were, we felt in the way, and it was a great imposition landing on them with three little children. They were in their late sixties and set in their ways. Anyway, it wasn't fair on them, and it was very hard on us after always having our own place before.

In those days, the Catholic church was left open all day and I'd call in to light a candle and say a few prayers, asking Our Lady to help me find a house. This one particular day I broke down in church and said to the Sacred Heart, 'Jesus, you know how much we need and want our own place, but if for some reason it's not to be just yet, then please help me to have patience to bear it and accept Your will. My life is in Your hands. I trust in You.' With that I lit a candle in front of the Sacred Heart statue and left the church. I remembered mom's words: maybe the house we were meant to have wasn't ready yet, but something had got to happen soon because I was having a breakdown, crying all the time.

As I left the church, something told me to try Hales

Properties, on the Chester Road, one last time. I had called in many times before without any luck, but they had told me to keep trying, as they never knew when one of their houses would become empty. I carried all three children up the steep staircase to the office above the shops. I must have looked a sorry sight with my eyes still red through crying in church, when I asked the receptionist if they had any houses to let this week. She hesitated and said, "Just a minute, we have had one of our tenants call in to the office today to say they were leaving at the end of the month, as they are buying their own house." She said she wasn't promising anything but if I could come back tomorrow when the owner and landlord would be there – and bring my husband with me for an interview – they would see what happened.

That night I couldn't sleep, excited at the prospect of having our own house. When I told my mother-in-law she didn't believe it, but then she didn't know about the power of prayer. We did indeed get the house and went to view it, as it was just a couple of streets away in Castle Bromwich. It was in a nice road and was a lovely big corner house with bay windows and a large mountain ash tree in the front garden; we couldn't believe our luck. The tenants were still in there and showed us round: they told us that they loved the house but the owner refused to sell it to them, so they had bought a similar house a few houses down in the same street. The lady told us that she would be leaving the carpets and curtains if we wanted them: little did she know how grateful we were, because we had nothing coming from Australia.

The day we moved in we didn't even have a chair to sit on. That Saturday I went to a jumble sale at the local church hall and bought two old leatherette armchairs for ten shillings and got the man to deliver them for me. Roy's dad had ordered a bedroom suite for us, but it wouldn't be delivered for six weeks, so we had to sleep on the floor till then. We borrowed the single bed that the boys had shared at their grandparents' until we got some beds for them, and Roy borrowed his dad's car to transport it in. Bit by bit, things came that we needed, and although it was a struggle to pay the high rent, it was heaven when I put the key in that front door, knowing it was ours. Thank you Lord, this is where you meant me to be all this time. I felt at home at last.

We paid £6.10 shillings per week rent, whereas council tenants were only paying £1.10 (before decimalisation) for a similar three-bedroom house, and because it was a private landlord, he could put the rent up whenever he liked: every year it would go up considerably. We had high fuel bills, as there was no heating in the house, just a boiler at the back of the open coal fire to heat the water, so it cost a small fortune in coal. It was a smokeless zone so we couldn't burn wood or any other fuel except smokeless coal, and that only heated one room. The house was all electric – there was no gas on the estate – and so we had huge electricity bills. We couldn't afford to run anything else except lighting and the electric stove to cook on, so it was a struggle, but we were happy. Roy had to do three jobs to make ends meet; besides his builder's job, he was a barman at the local pub, and a courier for Vernon's Pools Company.

Our Own Home

A few months after moving in, Roy caught pneumonia and was very ill. He had been working on the roof of a building in Coleshill in bitter cold weather and it seems that because we'd lived in a hot climate for six years, our blood had become thin and we hadn't become acclimatised to the cold. It took us a while to get used to the English weather again. He was off work for months; I don't know how we managed. As well as looking after Roy and the children, I had to do the school-run every day with Mark. There was a non-Catholic school on the corner of our street, but I wanted him to go to the Catholic school a couple of miles away, which was a 20-minute walk. I became worn out and anaemic, always tired and depressed. My doctor, a woman, gave me Valium tablets to help me cope, but after a while I became hooked on tranquilisers and became a complete mental and physical wreck, not eating or sleeping, and losing a lot of weight. It was hell.

Roy recovered and went back to work, but as his health returned to normal, mine was getting steadily worse. I started to shake and have hand tremors – I couldn't hold a cup and saucer without them rattling; my nerves were in a terrible state. I thought I was having a nervous breakdown. I had to sit up in bed all night because I was choking and couldn't swallow.

One morning, I woke up in agony with stomach pains and couldn't get out of bed. Roy called the doctor in who took one look at me and said he thought it was renal colic. He gave me some tablets saying, "If the pain persists, go back to the doctor's as you may have something wrong with your kidneys."

The tablets didn't work, so I made an appointment at the surgery and saw a different doctor that day. He was very concerned. He asked me to put my hands out, which were shaking as usual, and he called in my own doctor, who had been treating me for nerves for the last eight years. In a serious tone, he told her that he thought this poor woman (me), had been misdiagnosed.

"Look at her bulging eyes and hand tremors. What does that tell you?"

She just stood there saying nothing.

"Well, I'll tell you what I think it is: thyroid toxicosis, and I'm sending her to hospital."

Thank God for that good doctor, for he saved my life. I was being poisoned and it was affecting my kidneys. At the hospital, I had a blood test and was told that there were more toxins in my blood than they'd ever seen. The specialist asked me lots of questions about my symptoms, and about how I got on in the hot weather abroad.

"I couldn't stand the heat, doctor," I said. "It affected me very badly and I was glad to come back to the cold."

With that, he slapped his hands on his knees and said, "Now we know what's wrong with you; it is an over-active thyroid, which has become diseased and you have had this a long time."

He explained that the thyroid gland is a butterfly-shaped gland at the front of the neck, which is the master gland that works all your body, and to do that it secretes little droplets of hormones, which work every organ in the body – your heart, kidneys, liver, even your brain. When it is diseased it makes everything speed up, which explains why my heart was beating so fast, my bowels were always upset, my periods were happening every other week and my thinking was faster. I was quicker in everything, always on the go and couldn't relax.

I had suffered three miscarriages in the last two years

because of it and lost nearly all my teeth through the disease. I remember the dentist disagreeing with me about thyroid disease being the cause of my tooth decay, saying, "Rubbish. I have been a dentist for 30 years and never heard of that before. The only reason you're losing all your teeth can only be one reason, and that is not cleaning them properly."

I told him that I had a medical book at home that says the teeth decay early in the disease. He still didn't believe me and told me to bring in that book to read for himself, which I did. He had to eat his words saying, "Well, you learn something new every day."

I was beginning to lose faith in the medical profession. I could have felt bitter about that lady doctor who had put me through hell, saying she was positive that I was suffering from nerves and caused me untold suffering for eight years. I was starting to doubt my sanity, and feared I would end up in a mental hospital, like our Frank. There is no pain like the pain of the mind, and man's greatest fear is that of losing his mind, but tears are the safety-valve to sanity and I cried bucketfuls. The doctor at the hospital said he would try me on a drug called Carbimazole, an anti-thyroid pill that hopefully, would slow it down and get the heart beating steadily so they could operate. Once it was out, I would feel calmer and much better in myself but would be on Thyroxine tablets for life. I was so relieved that they had finally found out what was making me so ill, and could put it right. I had gone down to 6 $\frac{1}{2}$ stone in weight: that was the reason I was choking and having difficulty in swallowing, because I had an in-growing goitre making me sick.

When I eventually had the thyroidectomy, I was told that unfortunately because I had had this illness for such a long time, it had become cancerous. This was in August 1975 and I was just under 35 years old. I had been in hospital for over a month before the operation as they couldn't get my heart right, and they wanted to get me fit for the operation. In order to do that, they had to slow my heart right down, but every time the nurse would take my pulse my heart would race faster. They tried me on a new drug that calms you down so much that you don't care if they chop your head off. The morning I went down to theatre I was laughing and joking with the porter, who said, "Whatever you're on, I'd like some of that."

A strange thing happened to me on the operating table and under the anaesthetic. I had what can only be described as an out-of-body experience. While the surgeon was operating on me, I floated out of my body up onto the ceiling of the theatre and was looking down on myself, watching the doctors and nurses working on me. I could hear every word they were saying to each other. I wasn't afraid and it didn't last very long before I was back in my body and coming round in the recovery room. The nurse who was looking after me was the same one who'd asked the surgeon during the operation why he didn't remove the whole of the gland, and he had replied, "I can't, because it's attached to the pituitary gland at the base of the brain and that wouldn't work if I took out the whole gland."

I found out later that the pituitary gland governs growth such as bones, hair and even fingernails. I told the nurse about my experience while under the anaesthetic and she said, "No, it's impossible. You were probably dreaming, or just coming round."

"No, I heard everything you said to the doctor," I replied, repeating it word for word; she was amazed. Later on, I thought that I would never be afraid of dying if that is what happens. I know that we definitely have a soul; that part of us that lives on after the body shuts down. I believe that I died for a few seconds that day, but came back for a reason; my time wasn't up.

After the post-operative recovery period when I was at home, I collapsed and had to be rushed back into hospital, into the same ward that I came out of. They took some fluid from my neck and sent it to the lab; they told me there was something growing, some infection or bacteria, and my stitches were bursting open. I was in a bad way, even too weak to undress myself, but thank God they got me better from that and after a couple of days I was allowed home again.

I began to feel so much better, calmer and less agitated, and didn't need tranquilisers anymore; from that day I vowed never to go down that road again. The only tablet I have to take now is Thyroxine. Originally this hormone was taken from sheep's glands but now it is a synthetic drug. At first, different makes didn't suit me and it was trial and error until I found the right one: they all have exactly the same ingredients but different releasing agents, some faster than others, thereby speeding things up too fast, giving me palpitations and diarrhoea. Eventually, I found the one that suited me, which was Eltroxin.

I put on weight again, back to my normal nine stone plus, from the six-and-a-half stones when I was at my worst. After about two years I felt so much better that I got a job in an office as an invoice clerk; it was a well-paid job and the money helped out with finances at home. The children had their mother back to normal, and I was so grateful to have a second chance in life.

Illness

When you have been so desperately ill, you really do appreciate your health when it returns and you don't want to waste a minute. After working happily in my new job a few months, I was told one day that we were all coming out on strike for more money. I should stop working immediately, and even if someone needed anything, we were to refuse help of any kind. This was against my principles; I didn't want to strike. We all had to meet in the local public house at lunchtime to discuss the matter. At that meeting, true to form, I spoke my mind and got disliked for it. I told them I thought it was wrong to strike because we worked for a good firm, who were already the highest-paying company in the Midlands, this was Metro-Camel-Weyman, who made coaches for trains and had just signed a huge deal with either China or Japan and the staff was hoping to cash in on this too with a pay rise. I said they were being greedy and I didn't want any part of it. So because I had the courage of my convictions, I was ostracised and sent to 'Coventry' at work by everyone; it became intolerable, so I left. Just because others are greedy, we don't have to go with the flow like dead fish that float downstream.

I'm sure my grandmother was helping me from up above, and I trusted in God that all would be well. For another couple of years it was, but slowly and surely some of the old symptoms came back and by 1979, four years after my thyroid removal I was seriously ill again. The cancer had returned and had spread across my chest. The doctor who took the special x-rays looked grave as he told me, "I'm sorry to tell you that what you had four years ago has come back with a vengeance and has widely spread." I wasn't surprised.

I asked if there was anything that could be done, like another operation, but he said, "No, but we will try you on a course of radiotherapy treatment to shrink the tumour and prolong your life." I didn't ask how long I had got: I was in denial, thinking 'doctors can be wrong, I've seen it all before, and if they can't help me then I had got someone up there more powerful than them'.

When I got home, I cried, "Oh Lord, why? My children are teenagers now, and need their mother more than ever. How will poor Roy cope?" Roy's not good with illnesses; he's already fed up with me being ill. He said that to me one day, and who could blame him? I told him, "Tough. How do you think I like it? Look love, when you married me it was for better or worse, in sickness and in health, so OK, you have got the sickness now to contend with and I'm sorry." I used to struggle to cope, and tried to carry on as normal. Roy used to watch me struggle but wouldn't help; I thought he was being unkind.

Years later, when I was better, I told him how much I'd hated him when he had watched me carrying heavy buckets of coal in for the fire, and getting the ashes up each morning while he sat reading the newspaper. I was so weak, but determined to do it thinking, 'Pat, you're on your own, you're not getting any sympathy here.'

Roy said, "Yes, I know, but I was being cruel to be kind."

"What do you mean?"

"Well, I know you, and I knew that if I did everything for you and wrapped you up in cotton wool then you would have become soft and given up, and I would have lost you."

"Well," I said, "I wish you had told me that then, because I thought you didn't care and didn't love me."

When you have been given a death sentence and know that you haven't long to live, you experience different emotions and think of all the things you have never done, or will never do. I'd never flown in a plane, never learnt to drive a car and

I felt so sad that I wouldn't be around to see my children get married, would never see my grandchildren. You feel cheated and start to blame God, saying: "What will my poor mom do if she loses me, as well as our Frank? It's not fair."

When I was ill before, mom brought me a book to read in hospital. It was *The Song of Bernadette*, all about Lourdes in France, where people who are sick sometimes get cured. I'd never been to Lourdes; always wanted to go, but couldn't afford it. "That's it," I suddenly thought, "I've got to get to Lourdes. I'm sure Our Lady will look kindly on me. She won't see my children without a mother. But how? It's so expensive."

My mom wasn't strong-minded about illness; she was pessimistic by nature and every time she saw me she'd be in floods of tears. It would be me comforting her. Each time she visited she would tell me that I looked dreadful, and even said to the children one day: "The next time I shall see your mother will be in her coffin." That upset them, and Roy was very angry with her. I knew she was worried about me but, true to form, she never thought before opening her mouth.

At the cancer clinic the doctors couldn't help me. When I asked if there was anything they could do, the answer I got was: "Well, we can shoot you."

I told them: "No, don't do that because I'm going to Lourdes to be cured." By his attitude, I could see the doctor was not a believer.

He just said: "Get out of here," with a wave of his pen pointing to the door. This made me more determined to show them that I wasn't beaten yet.

I thought: "I'll show him. I won't give up."

That night, I knelt down and prayed hard: "Dear Lord, You know me inside out because You created me. Just as You cured people when you walked this earth, I believe You still can do it now. Just as I would take a broken old watch back to its maker to be mended, I am asking You to mend my broken body."

Knowing that I might not have long to live and do certain things, I decided to get in touch with my father if he was still alive. I wanted to get his side of the story and to tell him that I forgive him. I didn't know his address, only that he used to live in Sheffield, so I wrote to the council there, asking if he was on the electoral register and if they could help me. I put down his date of birth and last known address 30 years ago and waited for a reply. Within a few days I received a letter back saying: "With the information you have given us, we think that this could possibly be your father." They gave me his current address, still in Sheffield.

I put pen to paper, asking him that if he was the father of Pat, John, Carole and Frank, to please contact me, and I gave him my phone number. He phoned, and was quite emotional, saying that he had no idea we were back in England, as the last he heard was that we were all in Australia and he never thought he would ever hear from us again. We arranged to meet. I asked him if he would like to come down to Birmingham and stay with us for a few days and he said he would. I sensed that he was over the moon at this phone call and that he couldn't wait to see me.

So I met my father after 30 years; it was an emotional day. I had to meet him off the train at New Street station. When I got there, he was waiting outside the entrance doors standing there in his lovat green, check suit, orange patterned waistcoat and black bow-tie, and with his rosy cheeks, I thought, "Oh, my God. He looks just like a little Irish leprechaun." As I looked into his green Irish eyes, it was just like looking in the mirror at myself.

Mom always used to say to me: "You look just like your father; you have his Irish eyes." The others all had brown eyes like mom, except Frank, and having seen my father, I could see how much Frank had looked like his dad. He was the image of him.

Reunited with My Father

*H*e stayed for a week. I was curious as to how life had treated him, and was now satisfied; all was revealed. He was a very intelligent man who could do crossword puzzles in the newspapers in a flash. He was astute with money and had put some away for his old age, having owned a small shop for many years called Matt's Gift Store. He had a smaller, crushed nose from his car accident all those years ago, but as I got to know him I thought he's not the bad man that mom had painted him to be.

When I asked him why he left us all those years ago, he said: "I had to get out on doctor's orders. I was having a breakdown living with your mother; I just couldn't take any more and had to get away." He then went on to ask: "Did you know that I didn't want to marry your mother? She tricked me into getting her pregnant, and you were on the way – so it's all your fault." I knew that Mom was impossible to live with, and that it was true, she only married him to get away from home, where she was unhappy. But dad went off to war shortly afterwards and mom was left still living with her parents, and couldn't leave home until after the war when we moved into our own rented house.

He asked me how John was, and I told him that he was still in Australia, doing well in the police force and married with two sons.

"And Carole?"

"She's living in Germany now. They moved there when her husband Bruno had a bad accident and couldn't work as a bricklayer anymore. They went with their three children to live in Munster, to be near Bruno's family. He now works in an office, so with their five children and my three, you are the grandfather of eight."

"What about Frank? Did he ever get married?"

"No, dad. Unfortunately Frank is in hospital because he is mentally ill."

He looked angry. "That's your mothers' fault. She's to blame. That's how I would have ended up, had I stayed."

I said: "If you knew that, why leave us children to that fate with a neurotic mother?"

He said he was sorry about that, and there wasn't a day he didn't think about us all but he had to cut himself off completely and get on with his life. Selfish or what? He couldn't have thought much about us, otherwise he would have relieved our poverty and sent us some help.

But I mustn't judge him, and I told him that I had forgiven him. The week went by and he returned to Sheffield, but before he left, he told me something that shocked me to the very core. I was telling him how poor we were and went to bed hungry and if it hadn't been for good grandparents we really would have starved; my grandmother was a saint.

"Who? Lilly Rogers?"

"Yes."

"Oh, she wasn't your grandmother. Your real grandmother was Winifred Dyer, her sister, whom you called great aunt Winifred." I couldn't believe that. Lilly was the only grandmother I'd ever known and loved. No, she was my nan and grandad was definitely mom's father because she was the image of her dad.

"Oh yes, he was her father all right. He went to bed with his wife's sister and she had your mom. She didn't want the baby, and Lilly being the good woman that she was, brought the child up as her own, together with her own three sons."

"Did mom know this?"

"Of course she did. When your mom and I got married she was only 17 years old, and being under-age she needed her parents' permission to marry. Your aunt Winifred signed as her mother, and Tony Rogers, your grandfather, signed as her father. No-one else was at the wedding; Lilly wasn't there.

Well I'm aghast, What a shock. That explains why uncle Tony, mom's elder brother, was only 12 months older than her. He must have been a babe-in-arms when mom was on the way. Poor nan; and poor mom. That explains why mom was like she was, why she felt that her brothers were loved more than she was. Stands to reason that she was a constant reminder to my nan of what had happened; how could she possibly love her as her own?

When I told mom what he had said and asked her if it was true, she didn't deny it. She was livid with my dad; she just pursed her lips and said: "The swine," and that was the end of it.

I was sworn to secrecy; even my brother and sisters didn't know until mom died, and they were very shocked when I told them.

When mom found out that I was contacting my dad she fell out with me, calling me a traitor and a turncoat – how could I have anything to do with him, she asked, after what he had done? John and Carole said they didn't want anything to do with him either. I told them that before I died I wanted to forgive him and make my peace with God; bitterness and hatred eats away at you like acid. That is what happened to mom and it ruined her life. It is true that you can learn to forgive, but you can't forget. My greatest wish was that mom could find it in her heart to forgive the hurts, for if she did, she would be a much happier person.

Mom asked me if I had told my dad how ill I was. No! I didn't tell my father how ill I was, I just said that I had had cancer but was OK now. Mom got hold of his new address and wrote to him telling him the truth, and that if he wanted to make amends he should send me the money for Lourdes. He phoned me and told me about mom's letter, but I was adamant that I didn't want anything off him; that is not why I had got in touch with him. I had my pride. I had done alright without him all these years, and said honestly I didn't want it. I got the impression that he was relieved, and didn't want to part with it anyway because, as he had said before, it was all he had got in life, and he needed it for his old age.

I began to understand my mother better, and forgave all the unkind things she said and did caused by her bitterness at how life had treated her. She had never been happy and so couldn't give happiness to others. She had no friends because she couldn't trust anyone, and she disliked all Irish people after what my dad had done. For a while I thought the same, but later learned that Irish people were no different to English people, and that there are good and bad in all nationalities. Now, most of my friends are Irish, and I love them all. We must have cousins in Dublin because my dad had two sisters and a brother, who must have families of their own, but I have never met any of them.

Frank's Death

*B*ack to our Frank. We had lost count of how many times we were called to the hospital because he had taken an overdose, or was having his stomach pumped, or was being stitched up after slashing his wrists. Mom left him alone for a couple of hours one day and when she got home he was in a pool of blood on the kitchen floor after cutting his throat. This entire trauma was taking its toll on mom's health. She developed angina, and couldn't cope with him at home. Each time he was due to be discharged from hospital, she would tell the doctors that she couldn't have him home anymore, because she never knew what he was going to do next and was becoming afraid of him.

Each time Frank tried to take his own life, something would save him. He ought to go down in the Guinness Book of Records, as the man who attempted the most suicides. Mom used to say: "His time is not up and he won't go until God says so, because God gives life and God takes it away." Like the time when he bought a tin of rat poison and ate the lot; – but he didn't die. The doctor who was treating him at the hospital said he had survived because he had taken the natural antidote to rat poison when he washed it down with a bottle of lemonade. He jumped off buildings, and survived, and gave us lots of anxieties. We lost a lot of sleep over him; this went on for 17 years.

I couldn't do much for him, being ill myself and having a family to look after, but I did my best. He came to our house every week for a meal. He'd have a shower and some clean clothes and he would be fine when he first arrived but would suddenly change, like Jekyll and Hyde; calling me a witch because I had a black cat. The poor cat would be kicked up in the air, and then he would accuse me of poisoning the food I'd given him. I realised that it was paranoia and part of his illness, but it was distressing all the same.

He phoned us up dozens of times each week, at all hours of the day and night. He also phoned his brother, John, in Australia in the middle of the night, asking him for money. There wasn't much John could do, but I do know that he used to send money over to mom to help out. My sister, Carole, was also very good to mom, sending money over every week for years.

Because John, Frank's only brother, was so far away, Roy took over the role of brother to him and had the patience of Job with him. We got calls from hundreds of miles away saying: "Come and get me, I'm stranded with no money."

One time, he was in Graves End, London. "What are you doing there, Frank?"

"I just fancied a trip on the train." He had gone with no money and in order to get him back home, we had to pay his fare home, as well as his outgoing fare at this end before the station master would put him on a train back to Birmingham. Roy had to meet him off the train and drive him back to Rubery Hill Hospital.

Many times things like that happened: like when he and another patient borrowed one of the doctors cars and drove it away out into the countryside until it ran out of petrol, and poor Roy had to take them a can of petrol so that they could get back. Roy used to say: "I don't know who is the daftest, him or us for standing it."

When mom wouldn't have him at home any more the social worker found Frank a flat of his own. It was a nice little flat near to the hospital, but needed furniture and household stuff, which we supplied him with. As it happened, one of Roy's workmates had a lot of furniture for sale, as he was moving home, so we went and bought everything that he could possibly need, even crockery and bedclothes; you name it, we managed to get it for him, and we made it really cosy.

I remember saying: "Well, if he doesn't make a go of it here, he never will." I really thought that this might be the turning point for him, but it wasn't, and he only lasted a few weeks. Why did we trust him? We'd go up each week with a bag of groceries for him. One day, we arrived to find the front door kicked in and the flat empty, even the light bulbs had been taken. But where was Frank? He was back in hospital, high on drugs; this time in a padded cell. He had sold everything we had struggled to get for him; it had cost around a thousand pounds. He never went back to that flat.

When Frank finally succeeded in committing suicide it hit the front page of the *Birmingham Mail*: 'MAN IN DEATH PLUNGE DECAPITATED'. We had to hide the papers from mom.

Apparently one morning in February, in the snow, with little clothing on, he walked out of the hospital to a motorway bridge and threw himself off it, into the oncoming traffic below. A man who was walking his dog on the bridge saw it happen, saying he thought it strange on such a cold day that Frank was only wearing trousers, and a short-sleeved, cotton shirt. He looked back at Frank and saw that he had jumped. Every time I cross a motorway bridge, I think of poor Frank, and say a prayer for him.

The person whose car ran over him was a woman dentist, on her way to work. She said she saw what looked like a ragdoll falling out of the sky in front of her and couldn't stop in time, as the road was icy. Her Range Rover 4x4 went over him, I got her phone number off the police because they told me she was traumatised by what had happened, and I assured her it wasn't her fault. I explained that Frank was mentally ill and that he had tried so many times to end his life; she was just in that place when he succeeded. I told her not to let it affect her life and to put it behind her if she could.

I had the funeral to arrange and was worried that, because of the way that he had died, he wouldn't be allowed a Christian burial. But apparently the church now allowed it, as a Bishop had just published an article about the church's teaching that God won't condemn those driven to despair, and only God can stand in judgement of a person's soul. So he had a Christian burial.

The undertaker said to me, "No way will anyone be able to see the body. That should have upset me, but I've always believed that it doesn't matter what happens to the body, it is the soul that matters, and Frank's soul was at peace, at last.

In his lucid moments, he would tell me that he would rather be a man with no arms and no legs than go through the terrible torment of the mind; it must have been hell for him, thinking that we were all plotting against him. Nothing could convince him otherwise, and that we loved him. You hear of people being possessed by the devil – well sometimes it was just like an evil spirit was taunting him.

His last Christmas he spent in hospital because none of us could have him. I guess we were all fed up with the mayhem he kept causing; it was becoming unbearable for us too. Mom, as per usual, said something she shouldn't have, she told him that we were all fed up with his antics, and the next time he thought of ending it all, to make a good job of it. He did. What a waste of a young life; he was just 35 when he died. He was a good lad who got into the wrong company and onto evil drugs that ruined his life.

That was not the first time that Frank had made the front page of the newspaper. When he was 14 years old in Australia, he saved a girl, aged 12, from drowning. She had fallen into the Torrens River, near to where we lived, and it was infested with snakes; we knew that for a fact because Frank kept bringing them home to frighten us. One night he came in with one in a shoebox and asked me to have a look inside. I shot up in the air screaming – I was pregnant at the time – but he thought it was hilarious. The day he became a hero was when he and some friends were on a rope-footbridge across the river and one of the girls slipped through the ropes and fell into the water; she couldn't swim. He dived in fully clothed and rescued her. That same week, his photo was in the paper with a brand new bike that the father of the girl had bought for him, to say thank you for saving his daughter's life. A few months later, he received a Certificate of Merit from the Royal Humane Society of Australia. That certificate took pride of place on mom's living-room wall, and when she died, I took it. It reads like this:

The Royal Humane Society of Australia, under the patronage of her Majesty the Queen, his Excellency the Governor General and the Lord Mayor of all the capital cities on the 17th day of December 1962, it was resolved that the courage and humanity, displayed by Francis Anthony Murray, aged 14 years, in rescuing Marilyn McFarlane, aged 12, from Gilberton, from the Torrens River on 4 August 1962, call for the admiration of the court, and justly entitle him to the certificate of merit of this society, which is hereby awarded.

Signed by the President and Secretary.

So, his life was not in vain. He had been there at the right time for someone else. I doubt if anyone else would have dived into a snake-infested river to save someone; perhaps when he dived off the motorway bridge he was reliving that event. In the same year as the rescue year, he was in the newspaper again for doing exactly the same thing and saved a younger child from drowning in the same river; her name was Mary aged 6. Frank was on the footbridge which crossed the river. Three girls were playing on the bank when suddenly one of the girls slipped on the muddy bank and fell three feet into the water. Again, Frank dashed from the bridge and dived in fully clothed to rescue her. That was my brother in happier days.

A priest I knew came to see me after Frank's death and said, "Now Pat, I know what you are thinking, that because Frank committed suicide, he has dammed his soul. But that is not true. When Frank did it, the balance of his mind was disturbed, and he wasn't answerable for his actions. God is merciful and always ready to forgive. When Jesus died on the cross He died for all men, even Judas, who betrayed Him. Your brother was a good man by nature, I am sure he's found peace at last in heaven. Have some Masses said for him and leave him to God."

Poor Frank; I pray for him.

Lourdes

I kept in touch with my father and concentrated on getting to Lourdes, but with no money and three young children, what hope had I got? Down at the church one day, I was given a prayer card of St Jude, the Patron Saint of Hopeless Cases. Supposedly, if you say the 'Novena Prayer', (a prayer to be said at the end of each day's devotion for nine days), your prayer will be miraculously granted. I decided to give it a try. It went something like this:

> 'Oh holy St Jude, Apostle and martyr, friend and relative of Jesus Christ, faithful intercessor for those who implore your help in times of need, come to my aid in this, my necessity and in return I promise to make your name known and cause you to be invoked.'

St Jude wasn't the one who betrayed Our Lord. There were two Apostles named Judas and people often get them mixed up: Judas Iscariot, who sold Jesus for 30 pieces of silver, and Judas Thaddeus who was a relative of Jesus.

I said the Novena Prayer faithfully for nine days asking St Jude to help me get to Lourdes. Low and behold, a letter dropped through the letterbox from my sister Carole in Australia saying: "Pat, mom tells me how ill you are and that you want to get to Lourdes. Well guess what? We have just sold our house, the one we bought off you, and made a good profit, so here's 1,000 Australian dollars for you to go to Lourdes, and, take your Caroline with you."

Oh, my God, I could go, I had the money. I knew we would always share in our family: when one of us had any luck, we didn't forget each other, and thanks to my good sister, my dreams came true.

It wasn't that straightforward, however. This was in 1979, the Centenary of St Bernadette's death and everyone was flocking to Lourdes, even the Holy Father, Pope John Paul II was there, and there wasn't a bed to be had. I couldn't book a trip or a place to stay, as Lourdes was full. I didn't know what to do. I thought, back to my Novena Prayer to St Jude; he had helped me to get the money, now he might help again. Whilst saying the Prayer each day, I received a phone call from a nun called Sister Jean, who had been Caroline's teacher at school. After introducing herself she said: "Now, Mrs Brookes, I understand you are trying to get to Lourdes? Caroline has asked me to help you and I will do my best, dear. Each year, we sisters go with Kipling Travel in Hall Green, and Mr Grey, the travel agent, is a good friend of mine. I will ask him to be on the lookout for any cancellations." She went on to say: "Do not worry dear, if Our Lady wants you there, She will get you there."

I thanked Sister Jean, explaining that it had to be this year, as next year may be too late. It was September already, and Lourdes closed down for the winter in October, and didn't open up again until next Easter. I had less than a month to get there. I didn't know how much longer I had: the hospital had said the radiotherapy would prolong my life by months, but judging by how weak I was, I didn't even know if I'd hold up with the travelling while I was there, which is why I wanted Caroline to be with me. She was 13 at the time.

I finished the second Novena to St Jude, and sure enough, straight afterwards Mr Grey from Kipling Travel phoned me saying, "Mrs Brookes, can you travel in two days' time? I have two seats available that have been cancelled from London; one person is too sick to travel and the other one has died." My heart leapt, "Yes, I can go." We had to travel from Gatwick Airport and meet up with a group from a church in Essex.

Thank you St Jude for interceding for me and helping me once again. We didn't have a passport but that was soon sorted out with yearly ones from the Post Office. After paying for the passports, and our fares to Mr. Grey, we still had a fair bit of spending money and were set to go. All I wanted now was the energy to make the trip; I couldn't even mop the kitchen floor without collapsing in a heap, in a cold sweat.

On 2nd October 1979, Roy drove us down to Gatwick and saw us off on the plane. It was the first time either of us had flown before, and we were a little nervous, but if you really want to do something, nothing will deter you. Before leaving, I said to Roy, "We get back on your birthday, 5th October. I'll be bringing you a new woman for your birthday, love." He just smiled. Mom and friends were praying for me, and I knew Our Lady was with me.

When we arrived at Tarbes Airport, we got a coach to our hotel in Lourdes. We stayed in a large hotel, not far from the grotto, 'The Astoria,' which was choc-a-bloc. What I had been told was correct, there wasn't a bed to be had in Lourdes: even the priest from our group had to sleep in the lounge on a settee, and wash in the toilets; he wasn't as lucky as we were.

Caroline and I were shown to a bedroom with four single beds – we'd be sharing with a woman my age, also named Pat, and her daughter Denise who was the same age as Caroline. Denise suffered with muscular dystrophy and had been told that she would soon be in a wheelchair, as it was a progressive disease. She walked rather stiffly and kept falling over, but was a lovely bubbly girl, always joking and happy, and made light of her illness. Of course her mother was hoping and praying for a cure. Right from the start, the four of us became firm friends, and Denise and Caroline went everywhere together.

The weather was lovely and warm and it was a beautiful place. The first thing we did, after our evening meal, was to go down to the grotto where Our Lady had appeared to St Bernadette. I looked up at the statue in the niche and thanked her for getting me there. I prayed for the two people who couldn't be there, whose places we had taken; we didn't stay long that night as we were all tired after our long journey and wanted to get to bed. We did, however, watch the torchlight procession and join in the hymn singing. It was all wonderful; everywhere we went there were people in wheelchairs and on stretchers, all much worse off than me. There were hundreds of helpers looking after the infirm pilgrims; fetching water for them to drink and helping them get around.

Souvenir shops lined the roads, from the Domain to the hotels, selling religious items such as statues, rosaries, medals, books and videos. I bought a number of empty statuette bottles to fill up at the taps, and a large flagon, which I filled and carried round with me every day, drinking the water until it was coming out of my ears. We bought more small bottles at other times, ending up with a suitcase full of Lourdes' water to take home. I was worried that we might not be able to lift the cases and have to pay excess baggage at the airport on the way home, but thankfully we got through free of charge.

The next morning after Mass we made our way to the baths, waiting outside for about an hour, saying the rosary together. Once inside, we were ushered, along with three other ladies, into a cubicles behind curtains to undress, then a cold, wet sheet was slapped around my body, which took my breath away. The curtain opposite was pulled back and I found myself standing at the foot of a small oblong sunken bath just big enough for one person through which the miraculous spring flows, and it was freezing. Two French lady-helpers guided me down the steps, into the water, until I was submerged up to my shoulders.

At the far end of the bath a few feet away was a small

statue of Our Lady that I kissed saying a prayer asking Her to pray for us now, and at the hour of our death. After that, I turned around and got out up the steps and went back into the cubicle to dress. Then it was the next persons turn, we each go in separately one at a time, but there are several of those individual baths all in a row with partitions in-between, about a dozen of them altogether, half of them being for the men down the other end of the building. I glanced at the lady opposite me who was getting dressed and noticed that she had had a mastectomy, and thought, 'She's had cancer, poor woman; I hope she's cured'.

In Lourdes you find you are not on your own in suffering because there are thousands of poor souls, all in the same boat and many close to death. The amazing thing about the water was that you didn't need a towel to dry yourself because the water seemed to roll off you, like water on a duck's feathers, and we were dry in seconds. When we came out into the warm sunshine, we felt so fresh.

It was a wonderful experience, and I wouldn't have missed it for the world. We drank the water by the gallon; I was nicknamed 'the Water-Carrier', because I carried the large water bottle with me everywhere, even to the dining table, drinking that instead of the table water provided with the meals.

I did a lot of praying, and a lot of crying in those four days. One day at the grotto, I opened my heart to Our Lady, saying that if She made me well again, I promised to spend the rest of my life helping others less fortunate and be in Her service. My life would be lived in gratitude to Her and Her son, Jesus, because I could not die yet; my children and my husband needed me. I finished off with the words, 'But if it's not to be, dear Mother, then help me to have the courage to face what is to be, and not to be afraid of dying'. I really believe that everyone, once in his or her lifetime, should make that pilgrimage and sense Our Lady's love. It's a little bit of Heaven here on earth, and even if She doesn't cure you, as a loving Mother, She enfolds you in Her mantle and you feel secure, and able to face anything.

On the third day we visited places of interest; The Boley Mill, where Bernadette's father worked as a miller, but got into financial trouble and lost it. He and his family ended up living in a disused jail called the Cachot, consisting of one room where they all slept. As I walked through the large black door to the Cachot, I touched the wood and the latch that Bernadette had touched all those years ago, and I visualised her using that door and that room at the time of the Apparitions. At the grotto I touched the rock below where Our Lady stood, which was worn shiny like glass, by the millions of visitors' hands over the years since it began in 1858. All that I had read in *The Song of Bernadette* book came to life from my memory, and I was in awe of everything.

We sat outside the Basilica during the day watching the procession of the Blessed Sacrament, listening to the church bells ringing out, 'Ave, Ave, Ave Maria'. Before I'd left home, I doubted that I would have the strength to last out on this trip, but I was able to do everything, go everywhere and see everything I wanted to see. I didn't want to miss anything and I didn't: by some miracle, I was given the strength. Caroline enjoyed it too, having a friend in Denise to go about with. They would go off together sightseeing and shopping, while I was in church or at the grotto praying.

The night before we were due to leave was the feast of St Francis of Assisi, 4th October. We were all sitting at the tea table, having our evening meal, when I suddenly had a strange sensation; a fit of the shakes all over and then a thumping sensation up and down my spine, just like someone playing the xylophone from the top of my neck to the base of my spine. The look on my face prompted my friend, Pat, to ask if I was all right. "Don't you feel well?" she asked. Just as she asked me, it stopped, and I shrugged it off, attributing it to the medication I was on and side effects, vowing not to take any more of those tablets, that was the end of the matter.

The next day, 5th October and Roy's birthday, we set off from Lourdes for home. I had promised to bring him a new woman home; all I knew was that I was a new woman in my mind. I was on a spiritual high: I felt uplifted and inspired, and knew that I had experienced a little bit of Heaven in the past few days. I was serenely happy and ready to accept anything that came my way.

Back from Lourdes

On my visit to the cancer clinic I distributed the Lourdes water to the other patients, telling them where I had been and how much it had helped me and encouraging them to do the same; it seemed to give them some hope.

The week after I came back I had to have a radioactive Iodine drink. It was tasteless, just like a glass of water. I didn't feel any different immediately, but on my way home, I noticed that the fingers on my watch were whizzing round with the radioactivity in my body. A couple of days later I noticed lumps under my skin on my chest, as if the tumour was breaking up; maybe it wasn't, but that's what I was hoping.

The weeks and months went by and I was still 'here'. I was weak, but didn't feel any better or worse; the least little job took all my energy. Christmas came with me thinking that this would be my last Christmas; then another couple of months went by, and I was still 'here'. I was resigned to God's will by now, and wasn't worried about dying anymore; whatever will be, will be, I told myself.

One day, sitting on my own watching TV, there was a documentary film about Lourdes, with people who had been cured giving their testimonies. One man, who had been crippled and in a wheelchair when he went to Lourdes, said that he was sitting in his wheelchair watching the Blessed Sacrament procession go by, outside the church, when suddenly he had a fit of the shakes and a thumping sensation, up and down his spine. At that moment he was cured, and felt a strong urge to get out of his chair and walk. He left his wheelchair in Lourdes and has never looked back since.

I sat there dumbfounded. I had had the same thing happen

to me but I wasn't cured – or was I? Maybe I was cured, but mine was gradual. Why don't I feel any better though? Also, because I didn't think I was cured, I had that radiotherapy treatment. Perhaps I was cured but had undone it all by having what was left of my thyroid gland burnt out by the radiotherapy?

I realise now that, because no-one had told me I had been cured, I still thought I was dying, and still felt ill. The mind is a complex thing, and until I came to know otherwise, I believed I was still dying. Oh, I wish that I had not had that Iodine drink and had trusted in Our Lady more.

Some old friends of ours Pat and Brian called one day to ask how I was, and whether we would like to come on holiday with them. Every year they would go to the Isles of Scilly. They had this large cottage with plenty of room for us if we would like to go; it would do us good. We hadn't had a holiday for years, and for Roy's and the children's sake, I said yes, providing that they would sit me by the sea if the weather was nice, and go off and all do their own thing and enjoy themselves, because I didn't want to be a burden and spoil their holiday, if I took a turn for the worse. After all it would be my last holiday and I was keen to see the children enjoying themselves.

The lads, Mark and David, enjoyed it so much that year that they decided to go back the following year with Pat and Brian. Mark and David entered a 26-mile marathon round the Island. David almost completed the run until his legs gave way and he had to drop out, but Mark completed the course and finished third. The only issue was that, for the rest of the week, neither of them could walk and had to have their legs massaged every day with olive oil until the use of their legs came back.

While we were there, David came into our bedroom one night with an earwig in his ear: it was buzzing and driving him mad. Roy ended up having to take him to hospital to have it removed. Also, while we were there, we came across Harold Wilson's holiday home; and who should be standing in his bathroom with the window wide open, having a shave, but the then Prime Minister himself. We waved to him and he waved back. With all the walking every day I became increasingly out of breath, so much so that I had to be carried uphill, with Roy and Brian holding me up, under my arms. It was my 40th birthday that week and I thought, they say: "life begins at 40', but, in my case, it will be, 'life begins in eternity'. I decided that as soon as I got home, I would visit the doctors with this breathlessness; maybe I need an asthma inhaler.

When I got to the doctor's, I asked what was causing the shortness of breath. She said that is was probably anaemia. I told her that I thought the cancer had spread to my stomach, because there was a hardness there.

"Let's have a look," she said.

"If I didn't know better, I'd think I was pregnant," I said, "because I haven't had a period for months. Can radiotherapy stop menstruation, doctor?"

"No."

"Well, am I going through the 'change' then?" She shook her head.

"Could I be pregnant doctor? I was told that my baby days were over when I had my thyroid removed as, without a thyroid, your ovaries don't work."

"Out of the question," she said. I think she was thinking, 'poor woman, she is demented thinking such a thing.' But, after examining my stomach, she proceeded to examine me internally and went very quiet, not saying a word, and looking very puzzled.

She went to wash her hands and I asked: "Well doctor, what's wrong?"

"I reckon you are 16 weeks pregnant. The breathlessness is caused because the baby is taking all your iron."

What a shock!

It slowly sunk in, and it dawned on me that I was not dying; you don't get pregnant if you're dying. I must have been cured at Lourdes last October, and conceived a child after my cure. It explained such a lot; why I'd put on weight lately and felt so different. I should have known what it was, having had six other pregnancies – three that were miscarriages, We didn't prevent having children and I hadn't been able to conceive for the last five years, so this was a second miracle.

Then came the crunch. "You can't have this baby, Mrs Brookes."

"You try and stop me," I said.

"You have had radiotherapy treatment, which stays in your body for three months and you probably conceived during that time. This child will more than likely be born with brain damage. I suggest you have an abortion."

I stood up, still reeling from the news, then became composed and said, "No way. I don't believe in abortion, but this is further proof to me that I was cured at Lourdes, and I can't throw this second miracle back in God's face."

"Well, I want you to have some tests done, because for a woman of your age, there is also a risk of Spina-bifida and Down's Syndrome to consider".

"I'm not considering anything, doctor. No tests. I'll take my chances, and whatever I deliver, will be loved and taken care of."

I left that surgery in a daze, trying to take it all in. The doctor was the same one who had misdiagnosed me before: I just had to hope that she was wrong about the baby being affected by my treatment, and that everything would be all right.

On my way home that day, I called in to see a friend Anne, to tell her the news; she couldn't believe it either, and told me that cancer often returns. It did with her mother, who died of breast cancer; she thought she was cured but it came back again. I told her that my cancer had come back and I was cured of that at Lourdes, and what God has banished from my body can never return. I didn't know how I would cope with a young baby, but I would just have to trust in God.

I went home and waited for the family. They were all in shock, and dumbstruck. How could I be dying one minute and then have new life inside me the next?

My Miracle Baby

How did they all react? Well, Roy was very quiet, but happy for me. It took a while to sink in, but gradually he started making plans and it gave him a new lease of life too, for he'd almost given up hope, the same as me. He even made arrangements to buy our house, asking the owner if he would change his mind about selling the property.

We had a fishpond in the back garden. One day I saw him emptying it out, and with a pick and shovel, breaking it all up and filling the hole in with soil and turf. "Can't have that anymore with a baby in the house." He was ribbed at work and this one lad who came into the office, wondering what all the commotion was about, said, "What's up Roy?"

"Oh, I've got a woman pregnant." Roy was like a father figure to this lad; he was upset and disgusted with him, thinking that it couldn't possibly be me, as I was so ill, so it must be someone else. He said, "I didn't think you were like that Roy; how could you be unfaithful to Pat?" Roy told him that the woman was Pat.

Mark our eldest son, was 19 at the time. When he found out I was pregnant he was annoyed with his dad and wanted to punch his dad on the nose saying: "Dad, this is your fault. Don't you think our mom has been through enough?"

David, aged 17, said: "Oh well, I might as well throw my record player out of the window right now, because I can't have my music on loud as it is, without a baby in the house. I won't be able to have it on at all then."

Caroline 15, said: "Oh, I do hope it's a girl, mom, because it would even it up around here then, and I've always wanted a little sister."

Seriously though, they were all happy for me. It was all

like a dream, and I decided to just go along with the flow and take my chances, praying every day that the baby would be normal and healthy. There was nothing else I could do; I tried imagining that it was happening to someone else not to me.

One friend said: "Congratulations, or is it commiserations?" and I told her: "It is congratulations, not to me but to God, nothing is impossible with Him."

I attended the cancer clinic one last time, where the first thing they do is weigh you in the corridor, before you go in to see the specialist.

"You're putting on weight, Pat," said the nurse.

"I know, I'm feeding two," I said, and she laughed, thinking I was joking.

Once inside the consulting room, the doctor said: "How are we?" Strange that he said (we),

"We are not too bad, considering, doctor."

"Considering what?" came his reply.

"Considering I am four months pregnant!"

"Oh yeah," he said wryly, "and what makes you think that?" It was obvious he didn't believe me, and why should he?

"Look Doctor, if you don't believe me, here's my GP's phone number at the surgery where I've had it confirmed."

I told him about my trip to Lourdes, and that my cancer had gone. I thanked him for all his help in the past and told him that I wouldn't be coming back here again – and I never did. I left him sitting there with his mouth wide open in disbelief.

As I got to the door he said: "Well, you know where we are when you need us." With that I left that hospital never to return to that department.

Many years later I did have an occasion to attend that same hospital 'The General' for dental treatment, where my medical records were produced. The doctor thought he had the wrong Mrs. Brookes, saying: "There must be some mistake, because ten years ago this lady was terminally ill and shouldn't be here. I said: "I know, that's me," and I explained what happened.

The mind is a powerful thing: once I knew I was pregnant and cured, I began to feel so much better. As the pregnancy developed, I became tired and weary. I attended the antenatal clinic as an old woman, compared to all the young mums-to-be; I was in my forties and cancer had left its mark. I remember saying to the midwife, "I think it must be a boy, and that he's going to be a footballer because he kicks me out of bed each night and the kicks are so hard, they really hurt." She explained that the reason for that was in older mums like me, the womb is tougher and becomes like a taut drum, so the baby's kicks are more painful.

My pessimistic mother was so worried about me that she begged me not to go through with the pregnancy, as she thought my body wouldn't take it after how poorly I had been. In her estimation, this baby would be a sickly weak child, and how would I cope? She couldn't understand what I was thinking: that this was another miracle bestowed on me, and further proof of Our Lady's kindness to me, and that God can do anything. Where's your faith Mom?

I had no real problems with the pregnancy, just terrible tiredness, because I stopped taking my Thyroxine tablets as I did not want any drugs to go through to the baby. I probably shouldn't have done that.

The time came for my delivery, and more than one doctor and nurse were present at the birth. A group of doctors also turned up; whether it was because they anticipated complications I am not sure, but I think it was more out of curiosity than anything else. The birth was a long and difficult one, and the scissor-happy midwife cut me to ribbons to get the baby out, leaving me to be stitched up by a doctor, who, having seen me, complained to the midwife asking, "Was all this absolutely necessary?"

John-Paul, our son, was born, the biggest and healthiest of all our children, and perfect in every way. Roy had been called to the hospital at 5 am because I wanted him to be there this time. He had never attended any of the other children's births, and we decided it would be his last chance to have that experience. Bless him, he was near to fainting when the baby's head appeared and he wanted to leave the room but I told him, "Don't you dare."

It was Roy who first held him and started to think of names for him. Peter, Joseph, Martin, Matthew, John, Paul, John-Paul. The baby opened his eyes wide as Roy said the last name and Roy took it as a sign that was what it had to be, and it stuck. I never stopped thanking God for seeing me through this, and for giving me a perfectly normal healthy baby, as well as the biggest one yet – 7lb 6oz. During the birth, Roy was repeating everything the doctor said, 'It's a big one.' " It's a big one, Pat," and, "He thinks you have got an elephant in there." I laughed because when I was overdue and the pregnancy seemed to be going on forever, I would say, "I'm going round again, like an elephant that carries for 18 months."

There was almost 20 years between my first and my last baby, and Caroline was 15. It was hard starting all over again in my forties, but Caroline was such a big help; she was a second mother to John-Paul, changing his nappies and feeding him for me. If I had to pop out for a few minutes she would mind him for me.

She loved her little brother so much. I used to think that she would make a wonderful mother one day and this was good experience for her later on. Little did we know it would be sooner rather than later because – just two years later – she too became a mother. At 17 years old she came home one night and dropped the bombshell. Our David had taken her to the doctor's and had the pregnancy confirmed; she cried and said she was sorry.

You think you have done a good job of bringing up your children and teaching them good morals, but for this to happen when she wasn't married was a real shock. Her dad broke down and cried at the time; he idolised our Caroline and dreamt of walking her down the aisle one day in a white wedding dress. We told her that she couldn't get married in white now, because we had always believed that you had to be a virgin to wear white.

When her son Lee was born I was with her in hospital. I cried when I held him; they were tears of joy. She and the baby lived with us for two years before she did get married, when Lee was two years old.

Meanwhile, because it was another boy in the family, all John-Paul's baby things were passed down; the crib, the cot and baby clothes, all to our first grandchild, something I never thought I would live to see. Thank God she didn't have an abortion, because that would have killed me. Our tears were turned to joy because Lee was such a lovely little boy, as well as a playmate for John-Paul. After the initial shock, I did realise that she wasn't the first girl to be caught up in the ways of the world, and end up in trouble. Being a close family, we all rallied round to help.

Mark and David were both courting at this time, and when Mark told us he was getting married, Caroline said that she wanted to get married too. And sure enough, the two of them got married within a month of each other. Mark was married in the October, on a lovely sunny day, but one month later in November on Caroline's wedding day, the weather was dark and cold. She had a lovely white wedding, with Roy walking her down the aisle; she was like a beautiful princess. She had mentioned to the priest who was marrying them that she couldn't have a white wedding.

"Why not?" the priest asked.

"Because I have had a baby, Father, and my mom says it's

just not on."

"Well, you can go back home and tell your mother that you can get married in white, and that I authorise it." Another wedding that I have lived to see.

Within another 18 months, our David was also married and had a big white wedding in church; that was the three of them settled. Both Mark and David were very hard workers, like their father, and each had their own house to move into. Caroline managed to get a flat and then her own house shortly after. Roy and I were left with John-Paul, who incidentally had been a pageboy at all three weddings.

Caroline's house was just a short distance away from us and we saw a lot of her. In a short time other grandchildren were coming along, one after the other, and in a spate of 10 years we had 12 grandchildren: seven boys and five girls, all lovely and perfect – grandchildren that I never thought I would live to see. Thank you, Lord, for all Your wonderful blessings, because children are God's greatest blessing. And I guess we haven't finished yet, when John-Paul grows up.

Legion of Mary

The years that followed were even more eventful. When John-Paul was five and started school, I joined the Legion of Mary at our parish church. It is an association of Catholic lay people who do voluntary work for the church. When I heard about it starting up, after a talk at Mass by a young man who was a legionary doing a recruitment drive, something inside me stirred, and I became excited thinking, this is my chance to repay Our Lady. I still had not forgotten my promise to Her at the grotto; yes, this was the perfect way to help others and I would enjoy helping this new priest who had just arrived. Now that John-Paul was at school, I had more time to devote to the church doing good works; I was free to take it on now.

Once I joined, I quickly found the type of work I was most suited to – visiting the sick in hospitals and nursing homes. I also visited parishioners who were on the sick list: because I had experienced illness myself, I had a great deal of empathy. I could understand how they felt, and what emotions they were going through if they were dying; the fears that they had were once my fears, and I would tell them about my cancer and my cure at Lourdes. As well as rosaries and scapulars, we were given miraculous medals to distribute to anyone who would like to accept one, with a leaflet explaining all about them. I quickly came to realise how powerful those little medals were; they weren't called 'miraculous' for nothing, because wonderful things started to happen to those who had them.

I told people the story of the medal's origin and how Our Lady appeared to a nun, St Catherine Laboure', in France in 1830. She told Catherine to have a medal made, showing her in an oval light the image, with explanations of what the picture meant incorporated into the design on the back and front of the medal. On the front of the medal is an image of Herself, with Her hands outstretched, giving graces to the world, if only we would ask for them. The words, 'Oh Mary, conceived without sin, pray for us, who have recourse to Thee,' were around the perimeter. On the reverse side of the medal is a cross super-imposed by the letter 'M', for Mary, Our Mother. Below that are two hearts, that of Jesus and Mary, and 12 stars, representing the 12 Apostles and 12 tribes of Israel. Our Lady went on to make a solemn promise to those who wear the medal round their neck and say the prayer on the medal, "I will come immediately, and take them under my special care and protection."

I became amazed that it really worked and helped people, not as a lucky charm, but a sure way of Our Heavenly Mother's love for each one of us and as a helping hand in difficulty. I knew that when I placed one of those little medals, with blue cotton string attached, round someone's neck that I was leaving them in good hands, Our Lady's hands. What we could not do for that person, She could, because of Her promise, and She doesn't make idle promises. After all, if the Mother of God took the time and trouble to come down to earth to give us this instrument, She did it for a good reason, and why shouldn't we use it?

Just like She came to St Bernadette in France in 1858, She had appeared in France in 1830 to St Catherine. Wonderful things happen through Her; like the miraculous spring and the miraculous medal. I have witnessed many wonderful cures and miracles. My husband bought me a gold miraculous medal on a chain, when I first joined the Legion; I treasured that then, and still do, 25 years later.

I learned so much about Mary, the Mother of Jesus, in my 20 years as a Legionary and that by loving Her, I wasn't taking anything away from Jesus, because He loves His Mother so much, and He wants us to revere Her. Didn't He give Her to us from the cross, when He said to St John " Here is your Mother"? He was also giving Her to all mankind as Our Heavenly Mother, and She always leads us back to Her Son.

In my work for the church, I learnt that if you placed yourself at Her disposal, She would use you as Her instrument and lead you to people and places you have never dreamed of. I could write a separate book about all the marvellous happenings that I experienced through Her; looking back, I was living with miracles on tap. Our founder, Frank Duff, started the Legion of Mary in 1921 and wrote a book by that name: *Miracles On Tap*. After reading it, I quickly began to see what he meant, that nothing is impossible with God and Our Blessed Lady; just like my grandmother before me came to know, they will never let you down. I trust in them completely to solve all my problems, and am amazed at the way they sort them out. I have made many wonderful true friends in the Legion, including my best friends in Heaven.

When John-Paul was 10 years old, we took him to a Healing Mass, given by Monsignor Michael Buckley, a great, healing priest. I had been following this wonderful charismatic priest for a while, at different churches and didn't want to miss seeing him again when he came to St Theresa's church at Perry Barr, which was half-an-hour away by car. As I didn't have a car at the time, I asked Roy to take me after tea, but I didn't know what to do about John-Paul. He didn't want to come, as it would be a long Mass with another hour of laying on of hands afterwards, and he didn't relish sitting still in church for a couple of hours or more. I suggested that they drop me off and pick me up later as we couldn't leave John-Paul at home on his own.

Roy ate his tea and suddenly said: "Get your coat on, John-Paul. It's Holy Week, and we should do something extra, so won't you come with us? We'll all go." And to my surprise he said OK, even though he had been rebelling about coming earlier, and he did as he was told. What was to happen that night was phenomenal; he was meant to go.

The last time I'd spoken to Monsignor Buckley at a previous healing Mass he had said something uncanny to me as I was leaving the church. He had grabbed my arm and said: "You have had a wonderful healing," and I looked stunned. How did he know? Then he had said, "You mean to tell me that you didn't know?"

"Yes, I do know father," and it was left at that.

But this night, he said something more amazing that really touched me. After the Mass, he did his usual walk amongst the people and spoke to different ones, telling them things that only they could know. He was drawn to certain people and knew what was in their hearts. He came down the aisle and stopped dead at our bench, looked hard at John-Paul and said to me, "Is this your son?"

"Yes, Father."

"And yours?" pointing to Roy.

"Yes." Then to everyone's surprise, he knelt down staring at him a bit more, making John-Paul feel embarrassed, then said to me: "Tell me, what is it about this boy? Because I feel compelled to kneel. It is something to do with Our Lady. Tell me what is it?"

"Before I had this child, Father, I was dying of cancer and went to Lourdes, and was cured. Shortly afterwards, I conceived this boy when I was in my forties."

"I knew it," he shouted. "Will you get up on that altar and tell everyone what you have just told me! You two go as well," beckoning to Roy and John-Paul, who were both looking rather uneasy, as they were both shy. I can imagine what they were thinking, 'what's she got us into now?' Everyone clapped as I gave my testimony on the altar.

I said: "This is our son, whom the doctors said I shouldn't have because he would be born brain-damaged, but look at him. He's a perfectly normal healthy boy; nothing is impossible with God.'

All the way home, and ever since, we wondered what that priest saw in our son. I pondered it in my heart, just like Mary did, when Simeon told her in the temple that her son was special; at that moment, I knew just how she must have felt. Truth is stranger than fiction, and every word of this is true.

It wasn't all plain sailing in the Legion; there were many obstacles to deter me. As well as being a wife, mother, and grandmother to all those children with whom I was very involved, we had an elderly mother-in-law living with us, as Roy's dad had passed away five years before. She had Alzheimer's disease and was very difficult to cope with. Apart from that, my own mother had had a heart attack. I was concerned about her but she lived with my sister, Moira. I was glad that Moira was looking after her, because I had enough on my plate. I was becoming increasingly busy with my church work, having been made an officer of Senatus (headquarters), and had more and more meetings to attend. The calendar on my kitchen wall was always full of things to do; there was hardly a day free to call my own. I was doing recruitment drives, giving talks at Masses and helping to start up about 10 other branches in and around Birmingham, all of which needed experienced Legionaries to show them the ropes. I was like a juggler with too many balls and it was a job to cope, but I am so glad I did it while I could.

At the same time as all this activity, Roy's business was taking off. He was self-employed now, and had a factory unit on the Tyburn Road Erdington, manufacturing plastic windows, employing half a dozen men, albeit mainly family, who would go out fixing windows in houses and office blocks. I was involved helping in that too, trying to keep his books.

I loved the Legion, but didn't want to neglect our home life and was torn between the two. I spoke to a Legion priest, Cannon Ripley, about this and he gave me some good advice: he told me that, first and foremost, I was a wife and mother – that was my main vocation in life – and to give to Our Lady what I had left after doing my duty at home. I always tried to do that, and never neglected my family; I knew Our Lady wouldn't want me to neglect my family, so I had to try and get some help. The problem was that as an Officer of Senatus, I was expected to go to Dublin three times a year for a weekend to Concillium Headquarters, where the Legion began. This was to take notes of news from around the world, and reports of work being done, as the Legion had progressed and spread all over the world, with millions of members. The Legion had started from humble beginnings in Dublin, when Frank Duff, a civil servant, knelt down to say the rosary with a small group of people, asking Our Lady how best they could serve Her. Judging by how it flourished, She certainly showed them, and its success was proof that She was pleased.

Roy and I were leading separate lives, as I became more and more involved with my church work, and he with his business. He was also supporting John-Paul's ambitions of a professional football career. Roy would go with John-Paul to all his matches; he even helped the manager of one team he played with, by taking all the lads to Southport for a week's football tournament each year, where they played different teams every day. Roy would look after them and cook their meals; they all enjoyed it so much and looked forward to going back every year.

Somehow, things worked themselves out. I got help with my mother-in-law, who went into respite care for a week, once every six weeks, to give me a break. She was now in a wheelchair, having fallen down the stairs in the middle of the night. She had lost all sense of time and would get up at all hours asking for her breakfast, roaming around the house while we were asleep, leaving the taps running and the gas on without a light. After her fall, she didn't walk again because she lost her confidence, which really was a blessing in disguise. It was easier for me if she was less mobile because I had been pulling my hair out in frustration, with all the strange things she would get up to. She was doubly incontinent and would mess herself just as we were about to go out, or when she had just been dressed, all nice and clean. I know she couldn't help it but it was so trying. I took her shopping with me once, before she got too bad and could still walk, but I lost her. I left her outside a shop for one minute while I went inside to collect something off the counter, saying: "Wait there, mom, I'll be straight back." When I came out of the shop, she was nowhere to be found. She had wandered off and there I was frantically racing round searching for her. I was just about to phone the police when I spotted her in one of the shops. From then on, I knew I couldn't leave her for a second. She died aged 90, after living with us for five years. I certainly learnt patience during that time.

My Legion work was escalating, but I couldn't give it up. I was on a mission that I thought was so important and worthwhile. One day I asked Roy if he thought I should resign, because I felt we didn't do things together anymore and it made me feel bad, but he replied: "I know that if it wasn't for Our Lady, I wouldn't have you at all, so I don't mind sharing you with Her." That put my mind at rest. One of my colleagues said to me: "You must have a very understanding husband, Pat, putting up with all you do. I know mine wouldn't stand it." I told her what he had said, and that I felt this was what I was meant to do: how my whole life before had been fashioned for this purpose and how everything that happens to us in life makes us the people we are today.

Once, when I was due to go to Dublin for the weekend, John-Paul was poorly. I had had the doctor visit him during the week, as he complained of stomach pains and sickness, but was assured it was just a tummy bug. I told the doctor about his headaches and aversion to light and he said that it was migraine. I didn't know children got migraines, but apparently it's supposed to run in families, and as Roy sometimes got migraine headaches I accepted that it was true. Roy said he'd be OK and I should go, but I didn't want to leave him; he was only 10 years old. Not thinking that it was anything serious and that Roy could cope for a couple of days, I went. It turned out to be appendicitis, and by the time I got back home he was very ill and being rushed into hospital with peritonitis. I arrived home in time to go with him and waited as he had an appendectomy. I sat with him all night after the emergency operation. The surgeon told me he was a very lucky lad because it was more serious than they thought.

"Oh dear Mother, I was away on Your business when I should have been with my sick child at home." I felt terrible about that but, thank God, he recovered quickly and it wasn't long before he was back playing football again, which he loved.

Driving Lessons

*F*rom then on I started to feel guilty if someone at home asked me to do something and I was on Legion duty. My daughter Caroline, who had four children by then, would call to ask me to baby-sit, or collect her children from school, and I would have to say: "Sorry love, I'm working at the hospital this afternoon."

If I worked alone, perhaps I could have changed the time or day, but as we worked in pairs I couldn't change it; my partner would be waiting for me and I couldn't phone her. I had my own car by now, having passed my driving test at nearly 50 years of age – another major miracle. I'd had a word with Our Lady in my prayers, telling Her I needed to learn to drive and get a car because it was becoming difficult for me to keep up with all the work outside my own parish and that waiting for buses was getting me down. I started taking lessons but decided that it was too nerve-racking for me with too much traffic on the roads, so I gave it up for a while. For my 48th birthday, Roy bought me a little Austin Allegro car, with a card saying: 'Happy Birthday and Happy driving'. He said: "You have got to resume driving again; no excuses. You have got your own car now, and I'll pay for all your lessons."

I started lessons again and it cost him a small fortune, as I wasn't doing too well. A couple of different driving instructors more or less gave up on me because I had problems with spondylitis of the spine, and had difficulty turning my head, which made it hard to look for traffic. I also suffered with a frozen shoulder and every time I had to change gear, my arm was in agony; it was as if everything was against me. Although I have a strong will-power and loved Liberace. She played his records all day long. I had to rescue her on that occasion and bring her round to my house and phone her doctor to come and give her an injection to calm her down, because she was upset and suicidal. The final straw was when the paper boy knocked one morning at 7am saying that "the old man round the corner has sent me for help, as his wife had fallen out of bed and he can't lift her."

I quickly got dressed and went round, to find Blanche on the bedroom floor with a duvet thrown over her; Owen, her husband, had left her there all night. Between us, we struggled to get her back into bed: nothing was broken and she seemed fine. I went downstairs to make her a nice hot, milky drink and took it back upstairs saying: "Drink this, Blanche, you'll be all right now. I'll go home." Just then, she jumped out of bed, saying she needed the toilet, and toddled off to the bathroom. I stood there flabbergasted; if she could do that, why didn't she get into bed instead of lying on the floor all night? I told her that I was annoyed at being fetched out on false pretences, and being sent for when it wasn't necessary, she'd been having me on. But that was part of her illness. She was in and out of psychiatric hospitals for many years; with me visiting and taking her everything she needed, just being a good neighbour. I would like to think someone would do the same for me. I had compassion for the less fortunate, thinking: "There, but for the grace of God, it could be me."

So, I went round to see what Blanche and Owen wanted and was pleasantly surprised when they said: 'Pat, we have decided to give you our car, (a brand new Metro), as Owen doesn't want to drive any more after a couple of near-miss accidents. It is, however, on condition that you do all our shopping for us, and take us to the doctor's and the chiropodist and any hospital appointments when necessary." I agreed, and until I passed my test and got my own licence, Owen came with me. I had a good incentive to make me don't like to be beaten, I decided once again to give it a rest for a while.

During this period, one of my daughters-in-law passed her test and needed a car. I gave her mine, thinking that I would never drive it.

I used to argue with Our Lady, (if you can have a one-sided argument that is), trying to reason with Her saying: "Look, if You want me to continue doing this work then somehow I've got to drive and get another car", but She'd got it all in hand.

My neighbours, an elderly couple whom I'd befriended because they had no family, phoned me up one morning asking me to come round as they wanted to ask me something. What could it be? I expected they wanted some shopping doing or a light bulb needed changing, as they would fetch me for all the little jobs that needed doing that they couldn't manage themselves. I was like the daughter they never had.

They were both rather eccentric, in fact the woman, Blanche, suffered with schizophrenia, just like our Frank. I felt sorry for her. No-one else would have anything to do with them, and if they did, they would run out of patience with them, because whatever you did, it wasn't good enough and they would find fault with it. For example, they would ask me to get 4oz of cheese each week. They would weigh the cheese when I got back and if it was a fraction under or over the four ounces then I would have to go back to the shop because they were so precise in everything. I thought I had a lot of patience, but I was very frustrated many a time with them both. Like the time I had to phone the doctor for a home visit for them: when the doctor arrived, they wouldn't let him in because it was inconvenient as they were having their lunch, dead on one o'clock. Another time, poor Blanche was in the street in her nightdress stopping all the traffic, asking the drivers to take her to see the pianist Liberace, as she wanted to appear with him on the stage; she drive again now that I had a nice new car, and a driving instructor thrown in.

Owen was glad to get out of the house as well. I got lots of practice, and after a while felt confident enough to have more lessons with a proper driving instructor. This new teacher had a big Rover, but I preferred the smaller cars for parking. I was having trouble with my reversing in the car, the rear window was rather high up for me to see out of while reversing, and either I wasn't using my side mirrors correctly or something else, but reversing was my downfall. My first test came and I failed, due to that very thing.

Back to the drawing board. I wouldn't be beaten. I practised reversing in my own car and perfected the technique, but still wasn't happy in the Rover. I put in for another test in a month's time, and the week before I was out on a lesson, hoping to do lots of reversing in the driving instructor's car, when the instructor, Mr Jones, said: "Now, at the next crossroads turn right." By mistake I went straight on and got us lost. Mr. Jones said: "Never mind, carry on, we should be able to turn back somewhere." But the road went on for miles, with no right turns, so we ended up in unfamiliar surroundings; even the instructor had never been in that area before.

We got so lost that my hour was slipping away and I had done no reversing that day. My time was up and we had to get home. I said: "I thought we were going to do mostly reversing today Mr Jones – it's my test next week." He was quite irate. "Never mind that," he said, "I will be lucky if I get back in time for my next client." That put paid to that!

I can laugh about it now but it was quite stressful at the time. I prayed that I would pass my test this time. I wished I could do it in my own little Metro car, as I felt more confident in that and was more familiar with all the controls. I seemed to do everything right in that car.

The day came for my test, which was set for 11:30am,

with a lesson one hour before at 10:30. While waiting for Mr Jones to arrive, I swotted up on the Highway Code and stood in front of Our Lady's statue in my hall asking Her to help me today. But guess what? Mr Jones did not turn up. 10:45 came, still no sign of him, so after another 15 minutes I phoned his house, whereupon his wife answered the phone saying: "Sorry, he's not in, he is out on a lesson with someone else." I explained that he was supposed to be with me as it was my test today and he hadn't turned up yet.

"Just a minute," said his wife, "I will look in his appointment book. He has got your test date down for tomorrow, the 18th," she replied.

"No, he has made a mistake, it's today, the 17th. What do I do now?" I cried.

"I am very sorry. Can't you get someone else to go with you to the test centre? You can't go on your own as you need a qualified driver."

I was in a panic. I had no-one. The family were all out at work and when I phoned my daughter, she was out shopping. It looked like I was going to miss the test and lose all the fees that I had paid.

By this time it was 11:15am. I did wonder if Mr Jones had done this on purpose because he was annoyed with me for getting him lost last week; surely not, but it was strange. Oh well, I thought, maybe there's a good reason why I'm not meant to do it. I believe everything happens for a reason and I was soon to find out that reason. I just had to get my licence somehow though, because my arthritis was getting worse. My knees were bad and I couldn't walk far; I was getting just like my grandmother was years ago and I didn't want to end up like her, crying with heavy shopping bags in the street.

I had been reading a book called *Send Me your Guardian Angel*, which said when you can't do something yourself, ask your guardian angel to do it for you. We all have guardian angels, who are appointed at the time of our birth to be with us all through our lives and they very often steer us away from danger and guide us through life – maybe mine was steering me away from an accident today. At the hour of our death our guardian angel comes to take us to heaven, announcing that this life is over and we are now in eternity.

I went outside to get something out of my car, thinking I'd have to leave the L-plates on a bit longer. A neighbour friend from across the road had stopped to chat – she knew I'd got my test today and asked what time it was.

"In 15 minutes, at 11:30," I said, "but I can't go as my driving instructor didn't turn up." I told her what had happened.

"What time is it now?" she asked

"11:20. It's too late now anyway." I replied.

"Look Pat," said my neighbour, "Vic, my husband, is home. I am sure he would go with you. I will go and ask him."

The next minute out came Vic: "Get your coat on gal, you will make it. It's only 10 minutes down the road to the test centre."

So off we went. All along the road I was asking my guardian angel to do this for me, to help me and take this wheel for me and for goodness' sake to do the reversing around corners well.

We arrived at the test centre a couple of minutes late. My examiner was waiting for me on the footpath; I apologised for being late and told him what had happened and that I had to come in my own car. He went all round the vehicle inspecting tyres, mirrors, etc, and we got in.

"Oh Lord, I hope I've got enough petrol in the tank."

He could see I was upset and said: "Calm down, you will be okay." He was very understanding, it was just like sitting in the car with one of my sons, as he was only young, not like the elderly, stern man I had the month before on my first test.

Off we went, and by some miracle I did everything right, or rather my guardian angel did, because it wasn't me that day. All I knew was that I was determined to show everyone that I could do it, even without Mr Jones and no lesson prior to the test. I was slamming the gears in temper and was being very assertive, concentrating on every detail, using my mirrors correctly and I did the reversing as sweet as a nut. I think it was my defiant attitude that got me through. We got back to the test centre and I turned the engine off, waiting for the verdict.

"Well, Mrs Brookes, what do you do when you come to an unmarked crossroads?" asked the examiner.

"You change down gears, slow right down, look both ways and if it's all clear, you proceed across," I replied.

"Well, why did you carry straight on without looking?" remarked the examiner.

"Oh blimey, I did. I have failed, I know I have," I replied.

"No you haven't," said the examiner, "because you have answered the question correctly. I am pleased to tell you that you have passed."

I wanted to kiss him; I couldn't believe it. I had passed my driving test at nearly 50 years of age, after three years of learning. I had seen off five different driving instructors; one had died of a heart attack, (nothing to do with me as I was on holiday at the time), and when I got back, his wife phoned me to tell me the sad news, so I'd had to find someone else.

That was the saga of me learning to drive. Vic had been waiting at the test centre and when I got back and showed him my pass certificate he said: "Congratulations Pat, you did it."

"Well, I don't know about that, but somebody did."

Vic asked: "Do you want me to drive you home?"

"Oh no," I said, acting with bravado. Once I calmed down, I drove home. All the way back I was thinking about ringing Roy as soon as I got in to tell him the good news. At the other end of the phone I heard all the family cheering: "Hooray! Well done, mom." That afternoon I took 40 cigarettes over to Vic to say thank you; a packet each for him and his wife Phyllis. I was very grateful for their kind act.

Being able to drive opened up no end of opportunities for me. There was so much more I could do at home and church; it was the best thing I had ever done. So many people have benefited from me driving and I was able to do lots of good works that I wouldn't have been able to do, like working at the hospital for 20 years, sometimes twice a week. I couldn't have kept that up with two bus-rides both ways for much longer. I would think of all the years when I was ill and used to dream of being able to drive: well here I am driving all round the country now and flying half a dozen times a year – who would have believed it? I went on pilgrimages every year to Lourdes or Fatima or Medjugorje in Croatia (formerly Yugoslavia), the Holy Land, or Knock in Ireland. In the Holy Land I learned more about Jesus' life in one week than from reading the Bible all my life. Around this time I was the President of two different Presidium's (branches) of the Legion.

Working for Our Lady

*O*ne day, coming out of Mass, the parish Sister caught my arm and said she wanted a word with me, so I went back into church to sit down with her and listen to a telling off. I couldn't believe it: I wasn't a schoolgirl anymore, but that is just what it felt like. She said: "Pat, Father is very annoyed with you."

"Why?" I asked.

"Because you're working in the other parish and he wants you just in this parish."

"But Sister, I'm not doing it instead of here, I'm working in both parishes, and Legion headquarters sent me there, and I have to be obedient to them."

But she got angry and said: "It's got to stop."

I got angry then and told her to go back to Father and tell him that I work for Our Lady and I go where She needs me, and with that I got up to leave.

"Well," she said, "for your disobedience, I want you to write an essay on what it means to you to have a Religious Sister in the parish."

She must be joking, I thought to myself – who does she think I am? I'm not a nun who has taken a vow of obedience in adversity. I have a mind of my own and wouldn't be told what to do when I knew I was right. I humoured her, however, and the next day I presented her with my essay. To please her I wrote that we are all very grateful to have a visiting Sister in the parish because she is an extension of the priest, who needs all the help he can get, and being a woman, other women might welcome a female to confide in; I thought she was a great asset to the parish. She read what I wrote, shook her head and said: "It wasn't what I wanted." I never did find out what it was that she did want.

She came to our Legion meetings and tried to take over from me, the President, giving orders as to what work she wanted us to do, but that was my job. I said nothing at first, but when she started finding us menial tasks like baby-sitting and cleaning people's houses, I had to put a stop to it because that wasn't what we'd joined the Legion for; we had enough of that at home. Our work was supposed to be purely spiritual, and I said that at the meeting. However, it did cause a bad atmosphere between us, even though I had put it as humbly as I could – I would never be insolent to the clergy. But I had learned to stand up for myself and for others when something wasn't right: if I was wrong, then I would apologise, sometimes, to keep the peace. I would apologise even when I wasn't in the wrong, thinking to myself 'I know I'm right, and God and Our Lady know I'm right and that's all that matters'.

An example of this behaviour was when I went with a parish priest to visit someone in hospital, an elderly lady, one of our parishioners who was dying. He anointed her and gave her Holy Communion and as we were leaving, I gave her a scapular, because we are taught to do that in the Legion. When Our Lady gave the scapular to St Simon Stock, She told him that whoever dies clothed in her scapular would be saved, and She would come and take them to heaven; it was another one of Her instruments. I thought it was a good thing to do, but at the meeting, when we were giving the report on our visit, the priest tore strips off me, saying that I had undermined him by giving the scapular, because he had given her all that she needed. I apologised and said I wouldn't do that again, but was thinking to myself, 'Yes, Father, you gave her what you could, which was the ultimate gift of Our Lord Himself in the Blessed Sacrament, but I felt compassion with that woman too and wanted to give her something from Our Blessed Lady.' I didn't think that I was undermining him; I felt I was complementing him.

Another episode that upset me was when I was sent to a church to see the priest about having the Legion in the parish, and to ask him if we could come and give a talk at Mass. He said: "Oh no, the only one who talks on my altar is me."

"OK, Father. Will you ask your parishioners if they would be interested if we came and set it up here?"

"You're not coming here," he said.

"Oh, why not?"

"I'll tell you why not," he bellowed, "because you lot think you have got a special affinity with Our Lady. Well, you haven't."

I was taken aback a little but remained calm and said: "Oh, but we have, Father. It is there for everyone and you can have it too." I left that Presbytery thinking, 'Oh Lord, it's hard to be humble. I know I'm far from perfect, but please spare me these run-ins with awkward priests.'

Needless to say, we didn't start the Legion up there, but years later when that priest was moved to another parish, as they are from time to time, I heard that the Legion was in existence there and that a wonderful healing had taken place through the Miraculous Medal when a blind man in that parish regained his sight.

There were a few smacks in the face (as I called them), from 'Old Nick'. I came to realise that the more I did for Our Lady, the more the devil got angry and tried to deter me and cause me to be upset, and that it was mainly through my own colleagues. For instance, I was at a Senatus meeting with about 100 Legionaries present, together with the priest, when the subject of a leaflet about the power of the Mass was discussed (we used this leaflet in our work). The priest stood up and said that he didn't want us to use it any more because he didn't like it. He reeled off his reasons. As he was speaking, I was welling up inside thinking: 'I can't believe what he's saying, because the words on the leaflet were what I believe Our Lord himself would say'.

There were 10 reasons listed why we should attend Mass and I agreed with every one of them. I can't remember exactly how they went, but it was something like this:

1. It remits venial sin.
2. It expels the devil.
3. We feed our souls at Mass when we receive the sacraments.
4. We receive Graces.
5. It lessens our time in Purgatory.
6. We respectfully adore Jesus truly present on the altar etc.

This priest was saying: "Rubbish," after reading each one and finally at reason number 10: (At the hour of our death, the Masses we have heard during our life will be our greatest consolation) he said "Rubbish" again and tore the leaflet up. I was shocked because I was dying once and knew the consolation of Masses to be absolutely true. What is the matter with him? Why is he saying that? I thought. I waited for him to finish because I wouldn't interrupt a priest. I did respect all priests and would even lay down my life for them, but something inside me said, this is not what I have been taught and that by keeping quiet I would be sinning by omission. I couldn't contain myself any longer and when it was open to the floor for discussion, I put my hand up.

"Yes, Sister Brookes?" (We are all called 'Brothers' and 'Sisters' in the Legion).

"Forgive me Father, but I cannot understand why you are saying it's all rubbish. I know for a fact that the Masses I have heard during my life will be my greatest consolation at the hour of my death."

With that, little Betty Evans an elderly lady sitting next to me shouted: "And me."

Oh dear, I didn't want to start a riot, I just felt so strongly about this. After the meeting I got reprimanded for speaking against the priest and speaking my mind, something that had got me into trouble a few times. It was as if Our Lady was prompting me to say 'that's not what my Son taught'. Maybe I was too intense, maybe it was a sin of pride on my part. I know I am far from perfect but through my experiences I had become bold and fearless. What I didn't know at the time was that this priest was dying of bowel cancer and maybe his thinking was disturbed. In hindsight I should have spoken to him privately, not said what I did in public.

A year later, I visited that same priest in St. Joseph's Hospital, Coleshill when he was near the end. He had suffered a long operation on his bowels and the anaesthetic had made him blind. Despite being very weak he used to say Mass in his room every day – a nun would come in and set up the altar for him. My partner and I were asked if we would like to stay and hear Mass.

"Yes please." During Mass he fumbled for the water and wine jugs that he couldn't see and I got up and handed him the two silver jugs and he thanked me. After the Mass he said something to us that I'll never forget as long as I live: "Do you know that in my life as a priest I have said more than 18,000 Masses?"

"Really, Father. I bet that is your greatest consolation isn't it?"

"Yes," he said proudly. Shortly after that he died, but not before he had confirmed my thoughts of that day in Senatus.

I made mistakes and learned from them and didn't do them again. When I was asked to be a Eucharistic Minister on the altar, helping the priest to distribute Holy Communion, I took it very seriously and was scared of dropping the Host. I actually trembled at holding the Blessed Sacrament and one day had to go and tell the priest about something that had happened that Sunday morning. I was at home after Mass, cooking the Sunday dinner, when my granddaughter came into the kitchen to me and said: "Nan, I don't know how to tell you this but this morning at Mass my friend, who isn't a Catholic, went up to Holy Communion with me. I told her that she is not allowed to but she still had the Host on her tongue, so she went and spat it out down the toilet. Nan, Jesus is in the toilet!" I immediately got into my car, still wearing my apron, and went down to the church but it was all locked up.

I knocked on the Presbytery door and the priest came out. "Father, something terrible has happened," I said.

"What is it?" he replied. I explained what had happened, I was beside myself thinking I had to rescue Our Lord, because I really believe in the true presence in the Host. I must have seemed barmy to the priest, because he wasn't bothered.

"What do you expect me to do about it?" asked the priest.

"Well, get Him out," I replied.

"Then what?"

"I don't know. We will bury Him."

But he wouldn't even unlock the church and said he was taught in the seminary that once a Host is consumed or destroyed, it ceases to become our Lord. I thought that wasn't right because I had been watching a video called 'The Miracles of the Eucharist' that proved that once a Host is consecrated it never decays and lasts forever.

One story on the video was about a priest in 1730, in Sienna, Italy, who, on the eve of a big feast day, consecrated 351 Hosts for the next morning's Mass and left them in the golden chalice in the Tabernacle overnight. During the night thieves broke in and stole the golden chalice, tipping the Hosts out into the poor-box in church. The next morning the priest was devastated, more concerned about what the thieves had done with the Hosts. Three days later the Hosts were found in the poor-box and were rescued. They couldn't be used for human consumption as they were dusty and dirty, so he put them in a ciborium and put them away in a cupboard where they remained for over 50 years. When they were found, realising where they had come from, as it was common knowledge what had happened in that church all those years ago, the jar was opened and there were the Hosts, as fresh as the day the priest had consecrated them. Tests were done proving that they had not altered in the slightest. Later scientists did further tests on them and found that in each Host were tissues of a human heart, so how do you explain that? If you were to go to that church, St Francis' Basilica in Sienna today, you would find them on display, still incorrupt after hundreds of years.

I am not disputing that priest, but two years later he left the priesthood to get married and now lives in America. Don't get me wrong, the majority of priests are wonderful, holy men and it's because of these priests that I believe as I do, I have met such saintly priests who have inspired me no end and there is nothing I wouldn't do to help them in their work.

I met two such priests back home from missions in South America, where they had lived like hermits. They had been in a church in London for a while that was sold and the money bought a large house in Birmingham, which they were hoping to renovate and convert into a seminary for students training for the priesthood in Uganda. These priests belonged to the Order of the Holy Spirit and their young students would be coming over to England to be ordained into that order. They needed help to get the house ready. It needed decorating and furnishing and some building work: I thought I would like to take that on and add the woman's touch, and they were glad of my help. I got my son Mark to help with the carpentry work and the renovation.

Every week I would go to car boot sales and jumble sales, picking up bits and pieces needed at the house such as chairs and bedside tables, cushions and curtains; it was amazing how everything came that we needed, like magic it turned up. It wasn't long before we got it liveable and looking cosy. I was told 'no frills, no bows or tiebacks on curtains, and nothing fancy because it's not my house, it's a priest's house and everything has to be plain'. OK, fair enough, I can do that. But one day I decided to clean the front door knocker and letterbox with metal polish; they came up like new and then with a tin of red Cardinal tile polish I set about polishing the front doorstep. It was a boiling hot day and I was sweating with all the hard work but was pleased to see the finished result; it took me back to my childhood when I used to do that for my grandmother and it always looked nice. I went inside to tell the priest: "I've finished outside, come and have a look." Well he did, but to my dismay he hit the roof. He did not like the red step and told me to scrub it all back off again. "What did I tell you Pat? Nothing fancy, everything plain. This is a priest's house!" he cried. I couldn't understand why he preferred a dirty grey stone step instead of a nice shiny red one; all my hard work was for nothing. There I was with a bottle of bleach and a bucket of boiling water, scrubbing away until it was back to normal; I think I lost a bucket-full of sweat that day.

My son Mark did a lot of work in that house, making six bedrooms into seven by partitioning one large bedroom that had two windows in to make two separate rooms and putting another doorway in. He fitted shelves and bookcases onto the walls and we painted and wallpapered one of the small rooms making it into a chapel, with an altar. I have attended Mass there a few times since. Those two priests have become lifelong friends and have been to my house for meals. I am so glad I was able to help when I did.

Around this time I also met a newly ordained priest from Uganda who was from the same Order. I was asked to be his Spiritual Mother and write to him, as he was going to work in Venezuela, South America. I was also writing to an Indian priest in Kerala in India, who was also newly ordained. His name had been given to me by an old Irish priest out there who ran an orphanage. I had found his name in one of the church magazines and started sending parcels over for the orphaned children. I got great pleasure out of getting bargains at car-boot sales such as children's clothes and toys, but when I came to post the huge boxes off, the postage was more than I'd paid for the contents, so instead I would send the money, for which he was very grateful. This new priest had no benefactors and asked me to help him. I also got lots of begging letters from people who had got my address from his letters, and although I had a soft heart I just couldn't take on any more, and was warned to be very wary of such things, as sometimes these people are not genuine. I once sent £100 cash in an envelope that was stolen, because he never got it and he told me never to send cash, as the Indian government confiscates it. I sent cheques from then on.

We corresponded by letter for 14 years when he was in India, and now he is in the Vatican, furthering his studies and I get letters with the Vatican stamp on. Also we can now speak on the phone and by email. He is there for two years, so hopefully I will be able to go to Rome and meet him in person at long last, or perhaps he will be able to come to visit me, as it is only an hour or so away by plane.

His letters to me were wonderfully inspiring. He'd tell me about his difficulties in the monsoon weather where every day some of his poor parishioners became homeless because their poorly built shacks were washed away. He lived in a little fishing village and when the rivers were swollen with the heavy rains, the poor fishermen couldn't go out in their boats as it was too dangerous, and their families were starving. I wished I were rich so that I could help those poor people. When the Tsunami hit India, that young Indian priest had the difficult job of burying the dead. A few years ago this young priest's mother died and he asked me if I would be his mother and if he could become my fourth son. The Ugandan priest was also another of my Spiritual Sons. I used to look forward to both their letters and when I replied to them I would try to encourage and inspire them but it was me who benefited most from their inspiring words.

A few months after joining the Legion, I was sent to start up a new branch in our neighbouring parish, St. Anthony's, Kingshurst. I had to sit in at the meeting, teaching them the rules – talk about being dropped in the deep end! I hardly knew the ropes myself. To show them how to do home-to-home work, I would go out with the new members. At that parish I met a lovely nun called Sister Maureen who was the parish Sister and did a lot of visiting in the parishioners' homes. She took me to visit many families in the parish, some ill or housebound, others with domestic problems or tragedies, such as bereavements in the family. She taught me the correct way to visit people and to accept everyone as equal, never to judge and never to leave a house without saying a little prayer with the family. Her wisdom and experience was invaluable to me and through her I made many friends; everyone loved her and looked forward to her visits.

One day Sister Maureen took me to a family who had lost their eldest son a year before in a knife attack. His brother Peter, the youngest son, was inconsolable. He had had the job of identifying his brother's body and was so bitter about it he was making himself ill. He had suddenly developed arthritis; his body was all twisted and his hands were deformed with it. On top of that, the arthritis tablets had given him ulcers; he really was in a bad way. I learned from his widowed mother that the boy who had killed her son lived just across the road from them: he had got off on a technicality, as he was a soldier in the army suffering from battle fatigue.

Peter, would take a chair and sit outside the soldier's house waiting for him to come out and was threatening to kill him;

he would sit there all day. His mother was very worried about him and what all this was doing to him; she had already lost one son and feared she would lose this one too. Sister Maureen was lost for words and didn't know what to say to this poor young man. My heart bled for this poor boy and I asked Our Lady to help me to help him: "Look what he's doing to himself." These words were given to me from a book I had been reading the night before called, *The Poem of the Man God*, by Maria Valtorta, the most wonderful book I have ever read, where I read that St Peter said to Jesus: "Lord, don't have anything to do with Mary Magdalene, she is a prostitute and I hate her," and Jesus said: "Peter, never hate, because when you hate then you lose my love." Jesus loved the sinner, not the sin.

As this boy's name was Peter, I repeated Our Lord's words to him: "Peter, do not hate because then, you lose God's love. Can't you see what all this bitterness and hatred is doing to you? It's making you ill. Hatred burns like acid and if you could possibly find it in your heart to forgive, you would become well again."

He replied: "Don't talk to me about God and forgiveness, I hate that man who killed my brother and if I get the chance I am going to kill him."

"Oh Peter, isn't it enough punishment for that man to live with murder on his conscience? For your poor mom's sake, who is very worried about you and doesn't need this on top of losing your brother. She needs you to be strong to look after her now; you are the man of the house."

But he was adamant that he hated God and would never go to church again. We left that house wondering if anything I had said would sink in. I left a couple of Miraculous Medals with them and the mother put one round her neck, but I don't know if Peter ever did the same. All I knew was if he could learn to forgive, his arthritis would clear up and he wouldn't need all those drugs that were causing ulcers, and that they would clear up too.

Christmas came a couple of months later and I was at Midnight Mass at my own church. I couldn't help admiring a man's voice behind me singing all the carols very loud, but it wasn't until the Sign of Peace, where we shake hands with everyone and I turned around to say: "Peace be with you," that I recognised, to my amazement, that the young man singing was Peter. That was a lovely Christmas present to me, to see him at Mass and reconciled to God.

After Mass I went up to him and said: "Peter, what are you doing here? It's lovely to see you."

"I thought I would sneak out to a different church where no-one knows me, so I decided to come here in secret. I didn't know this was your parish, Pat."

I smiled. "Well, I'm so glad you did and please keep it up."

Years later, it was Sister Maureen's leaving party – she was being moved to another parish in Somerset – and who should be there but Peter and his mother. He looked a completely different chap, older but healthy and strong, he had put on weight and wasn't crippled with arthritis any more, and his hands were not deformed and twisted like they used to be. I couldn't get over the transformation. He was wearing a medal round his neck, a gold one. At closer inspection, I saw it was a Miraculous Medal, "Gee, look what Our Lady has done now!" That was only one of the hundreds of miracles I have witnessed in my life; many people who were at death's door have recovered after wearing the Medal.

Another family that I was introduced to by a nun was a family whose daughter was pregnant at 16. The mother said she was too young and wanted her to have an abortion. The nun said: "We have got to do something about that, Pat, try to persuade her to keep the baby."

"I will Sister."

I don't believe in abortion, I think it's murder, but the young girl was being pressurised by her family to get rid of it. I had experienced what the mother of the girl was going through: the shock of her young daughter's pregnancy. I reasoned with her not to be too hard on her daughter and reminded her that her daughter was in trouble and afraid, and needed her family's love and that one day soon, just like me, her tears will turn to Joy. I said to her: "When you hold that little bundle in your arms you will see that every child is sent by God, and for a reason. Don't tell her to abort it; it is a soul from the moment of conception. You will cope, you will see. She's not the first girl to get into trouble and certainly won't be the last and it's not such a disgrace today. Unfortunately we don't live in a perfect world where everything we dream about comes true. Yes, we would like our children to grow up with no problems, but believe me there's worse things than having babies; your daughter's not dying with cancer or got AIDS, so stop fretting." The look on the mother's face told me that she was grateful for the chat and the young girl kissed me goodbye. Sometimes, when in trouble all it takes is to talk to one who's been through the same thing.

Hospital Visitations

*A*t Heartlands Hospital, the hospital chaplain, Father Anton, used to give us a dozen names of patients to visit each week in the different wards, providing us with a short explanation about each one, such as 'this lady's had a serious operation so don't tire her'; or 'this one has cancer'; or 'this man's had his leg amputated'; and 'don't be surprised if John nods off while talking to him because he has sleep apnoea'. We visited people with AIDS and infectious diseases, but I wasn't nervous about that. It was the same when visiting people in prison – they were so grateful for a chat, a magazine and not to be judged.

Before going to the wards we would pay a visit to the chapel on the ground floor, and say a little prayer, asking for guidance and wisdom to know what to say to the sick patients. As Legionaries, representing Mary we were taught to imitate Her as a loving mother, with compassion for each person. I would look on a young man as one of my own sons, and an elderly woman as my mother or grandmother.

There were some comical episodes in that hospital, because you meet all sorts. One time I visited this elderly man who had his eyes shut, but wasn't asleep: he was just resting. I touched his arm and said: "Joe, it's Pat from the Catholic church." With that, he opened his eyes wide, rubbed them as if he couldn't believe what he was seeing, then jumped out of bed, hugged and kissed me, then proceeded to do a dance, well more of an Irish jig, round the bay of the ward. Apparently he had misheard what I had said and thought I'd said: "Joe, it's your sister Pat from Christchurch, New Zealand," his long-lost sister who had promised to come and take him home. I must have looked like his sister and I had a hard time convincing him that wasn't the case.

The nurses came running to see what the all commotion was about. Joe was shouting: "Nurse, Nurse, this is my sister Pat, from New Zealand and I'm going home." I explained that it was not true and that he was mistaken.

"Well, whoever you are," said the nurse, "you have done him the power of good, because he'd given up and not left his bed for weeks."

The nurse then turned to Joe: "No more bed rest for you, you can sit out in your chair now."

Poor man, what a disappointment for him realising I wasn't his sister. I hope he didn't have a relapse and take to his bed again.

Another amusing story was when we visited an old man of 94 who had come into hospital for a gall bladder operation. He was a proper comedian, always joking; the nurses said he was a joy to look after. He spent all his waking hours writing poetry and one of his poems was pinned up on the wall above his bed. I read it and thought it was so good that I photocopied it and read it out at our meeting, to everyone's amusement. It was called, 'Life in Ward Nine', and went something like this:

> I came to Ward Nine in a terrible way, didn't think I would last the day,
> Pains in my belly and pains in my guts, I tell you I thought I was going nuts.
> The doctor came at home and said, get into hospital or you'll soon be dead,
> These angels of mercy, did all that they could, salt of the earth, couldn't be better,
> I'll write Tony Blair with a suitable letter.

It went on all in rhyme about his operation to remove his gall bladder finishing off with:

'Grateful thanks from your old friend Walter aged 94 and three quarters.'

We always had an amusing story to tell at our praesidium; we were a happy bunch, and looked forward to our Tuesday night meetings. Each week someone would report on an amusing incident, but it was mainly me who kept them all in stitches, like the time I had to give my report about crowd contact in the Birmingham Bull Ring shopping precinct, speaking to shoppers and evangelising.

We used to say the rosary down there every Saturday and some Catholic shoppers would come and join in. I had been there the previous Saturday, and when I gave my report about what took place, the priest, who was present at the meeting, nearly fell off his chair with laughter. I started off with: "I'm not going to that Bull Ring again, you get more than you bargain for down there. I tell you it's a dangerous place for a woman on her own."

"Why, what happened?"

"Well, I was mixing with the crowd and got caught up with some winos and alcoholics who gather there, and this Polish man, who worse for drink, seemed as if he wanted to talk. I asked him if he was a Catholic and he said he was, and then I said: Have you ever been to St Michael's church in the city? It is very popular with the Polish people as there is a very nice Polish priest who says Mass in Polish for them." He seemed interested and beckoned me to come closer. Thinking that he wanted to tell me something, I stood closer to him where upon he put his hand up my skirt and pinched my bottom hard."

That had never happened to me before and I didn't quite know what to do.

"What did you say to him, Pat?" asked the priest.

"Well, I wanted to slap his face, and call him a dirty old drunk but I just said 'don't do that' and pushed him away.

Oh, why does everything happen to me?" Everyone laughed out loud.

Another time in the Bull Ring, we met a man named Michael Finnegan, and I sang that rhyme to him: "I knew a man named Michael Finnegan, he grew whiskers on his chin again, the wind came out and blew them in again, poor old Michael Finnegan." I couldn't resist that but he started to cry, tears filled his eyes as if he remembered someone else who used to sing that to him – maybe his parents – and I was thinking I shouldn't have done that.

Yet another embarrassing episode that happened to me there while I was working, talking to the crowd, was when one of my colleagues came over to me asking if I lived anywhere near Shard End.

"Yes, not far," I replied.

"Have you got your car with you?"

"Yes, I'm parked over there in the multi-storey car park."

"Well, we have a man over there who is very distressed because he has lost his wife and we were wondering if you would take him home, as he's in no fit state to go on a bus."

I agreed and went over to meet the man and took him to my car, which was on the fifth floor. The lifts had broken down, so there I was with a huge, one-eyed, blind-drunk West Indian man, who was sobbing all the way and falling down every few steps of the five flights of stairs. Oh Boy, if my husband could see me now, I'd be out of the Legion quick sharp. I don't get embarrassed easily, I've always said I don't care what other people think, but I was getting some funny stares from people that day as if they were thinking, what's she doing with him? I don't half get myself into some situations.

Driving home with this man, I asked him: "What happened to your wife?"

"Oh, she ate a crab from the fish market and it poisoned her."

Through his tears he asked me if it was a sin to kill yourself because he couldn't live without her and was contemplating suicide. I told him: "Yes, it is and you mustn't think of doing such a thing. You must channel your life differently now and do something worthwhile with it, because your wife wouldn't want you to be like this. Why don't you join a club that helps people?"

He said he'd always wanted to help the missions abroad and do good works. "There you are, then why don't you?" He said he would think about it. I dropped him off at home telling him to keep in touch with the Legion; we were only round the corner if he needed help. He said he would.

On my way home, when I thought of what I'd done: picked up a complete stranger and taken him home in my car. He could have been mentally ill or a murderer, for all I knew, and anything could have happened to me. I was too trusting, but somehow always felt safe when I was on Our Lady's work. Like the time I had to go to St Mary's church in Wednesbury but didn't know how to get there. My partner, Josie, was a good navigator, so she read the map along the way. We said a little prayer for Our Lady to guide us safely there, as I had only recently passed my driving test and hadn't been on a motorway before. It started raining heavily and we had to keep stopping to get our bearings.

All we knew was the name of the church and the road it was in – it was one of those instances where a 'Sat Nav' would have come in handy, but they hadn't been invented then. It was raining so hard that we could hardly see out of the windows, even with the windscreen wipers on full power, so I stopped the car and said to Josie: "Wind your window down and see if you can find out where we are. What's the name of this street?"

"I don't believe it Pat, it's St Mary-on-the-hill Road and there is the church." We had stopped right outside our destination; Our Lady had led us right to the door.

Josie and I often reminisce about that when we chat on the phone. Josie is blind now and lives on her memories; they were happy days in the Legion. She and her best friend Beatrice had joined after they both became widows and said it was the best thing they'd ever done.

The Legion attracts people from all walks of life but they all have one thing in common, that of loving God and our fellow man. Just as Jesus chose his disciples from all walks of life, so Our Lady chooses us to do Her work on earth Each one has a different talent to give: one might be a good speaker; another a good listener; their whole lives prior to joining have been fashioned for that purpose, making them the kind of person that they are. All God wants is willing souls in which to work.

I'd think of the little boy in the gospel with the loaves and fishes who gave what he had so that Our Lord could feed the hungry thousands. He could have said: "No, I need them for my family," but he didn't, he gave it willingly so that Jesus could multiply them. It is the same with us: give what we have and watch the way He works, like the ripples on a pond when we toss a stone into it. My mother used to say: "Cast your bread upon the water and watch it come back to you a hundred fold." How true. Sometimes years after I'd done someone a good turn, the tables turned and that person came to my rescue. Sometimes I had gone without to help someone and out of the blue some good fortune would come my way to pay me back – not that I wanted paying back or a reward. God pays debts without coins, and He loves a cheerful giver.

One book that changed my life was T*he Power of Positive Thinking* by Norman Vincent Peale, who had the right concept of how the mind governs the body. Think negative thoughts and negative things happen, but think positively and never give up on prayer, and watch the miracles happen.

Hospital work was where I felt most at home. I believe

in the saying that 'laughter is the best medicine, and you can laugh yourself back to health', so I used to tell the patients jokes or funny stories. One woman on the ward was complaining about the doctors and nurses who would not tell her anything, such as how long she would be in hospital when she wanted to go home, so I said: "I'll tell you what to do: you go out to the phone box and ring up the ward and enquire how you are, saying can you tell me how Mrs Smith is on ward four?" The nurse will probably say she is comfortable and had a good night and maybe going home tomorrow, and when they ask who is calling, say: "Oh, it's Mrs Smith on ward four, only they don't tell you anything in here. Thank you very much." That always got a laugh, but I would urge them to receive the sacraments because Holy Communion is by far the best medicine.

One day Father Anton said: "Here is your list – go to Mrs Holmes on ward 20 first, because she is not expected to last the day." He had just come from giving her the last rites. "She has a brain haemorrhage and is in a coma, all her family are with her and they might appreciate you saying a few prayers with them." This was the first person we had visited who was near to dying and just before this I had come across some prayer leaflets in church with a prayer for the dying and had picked some up. My bag was full of different holy pictures and prayer cards. I would ask patients: "Who is your favourite saint?" and if they said St Theresa, St Francis, St Anthony, I would search for a picture of that saint to give to them, and they really appreciated them, as well as the plastic rosary beads I would give them, if they had forgotten to bring theirs from home.

The prayer leaflet for the dying was called 'The Divine Mercy Chaplet' and had a picture of Jesus on the front as he appeared to a Polish nun, Sister Faustina, (now a saint) in the late '30s and '40s in Poland, giving her this prayer saying: "Whoever will recite it, will receive great mercy at the hour of death," which means that when anyone says this prayer in the presence of the dying, He promises to stand between His Father and that person, not as the Just Judge but as a Merciful Saviour. He went on to say: "Through this chaplet, you will obtain everything if what you ask is compatible with my will."

I thought this was the ideal time to try this prayer out. I gave one each to the family and together we all said that prayer at Mrs Holmes' bedside, they seemed grateful for that, especially when I told them the story and how powerful it could be. Before we left, I put a medal around the dying woman's neck and left that side-room thinking that's the last we'd see of Mrs Holmes.

A week later, we were doing our rounds in that same ward and who should be sitting out of bed eating her dinner but Mrs Holmes. Time and time again I left that hospital thinking prayers really work and the Holy Spirit does guide you if you ask Him. I often thought,' was that really me in there saying all those wonderful things to that person and did that lady in the next bed really say she wanted to become a Catholic after listening to me? Well, I guess in order to be convincing, you first of all have to be sold on the product you are trying to sell, and I always believe what I say.

A woman in the next bed called us back saying that she had always wanted to become a Catholic, ever since her sister went to Lourdes when she was dying with cancer. She had come back so full of the place, telling her all about it and how it changed her attitude to dying and death; she died peacefully after that.

"Now I'm dying with emphysema, will you help me?"

"Of course we will. Would you like us to ask the Catholic Priest to visit you?"

"Yes please."

"What's your name?"

"Elsie." With that we found Father Anton and told him

what had happened.

"Wonderful," he said. "Leave it to me." This lady wasn't on our list because we had found her by accident, but believe me this was no accident, and as the story unfolds you will see why.

A few days later we got a phone-call asking Cathy my partner and I to go up to the hospital, as
   Elsie was being received into the church at 3pm that afternoon and would be receiving her first Holy Communion and Confirmation that same day. Could we be her sponsors? 'That was quick,' I thought, 'Father Anton has lost no time – perhaps it's because Elsie didn't have long to live.' She recovered enough to go home to die, lasting another couple of months with us Legionaries visiting her at home every week and becoming friends.

We took her a picture of the Sacred Heart, which she treasured and hung on her bedroom wall. She told us that becoming a Catholic was the best thing she had ever done, because if she hadn't, she would never have had such nice visitors. The night before she died, I happened to be in the area and popped in to see her at home. She was in her last agony and very distressed, and needed assurance that she would go to heaven. I told her that she was a very lucky woman because when she was baptised in hospital a few weeks ago, all her past sins were washed away and she was pure enough for heaven, especially with the suffering she had been through in recent weeks. She had a clean soul, ready for heaven and I told her not to be afraid because she was going straight there where she would meet loved ones, like her sister, who had died before her. She died the following day.

At her funeral, waiting outside the crematorium to go in, I noticed an old friend of the family in the crowd – his wife, who had passed away a few years ago, was a friend of mine. I went over to speak to him.

"Hello Cyril, what brings you here?"

"Oh my sister-in-law died." I told him we were there for the funeral of a lady named Elsie whom we'd met in hospital with emphysema.

"That's her," he said. "That is my sister-in-law, Ellen's sister."

"You mean Ellen, my friend who went to Lourdes with me before she died? I didn't know I was visiting her sister. Oh my God, she'd told me that her sister had cancer and went to Lourdes before she died but I never connected them. How strange I never dreamt of putting two and two together."

After the funeral I was in a daze, thinking it was as if my friend Ellen, 'up there', had somehow been getting me to help her sister, just as I had helped her. I remember after our trip to Lourdes, Ellen had told me that her granddaughter loved hearing all about the trip and about St Bernadette and had told her RE teacher at school about it. The teacher asked if her grandmother would consider coming into school and to give a talk to the class of 15- and 16-year-olds. Ellen had said: "I could never stand up in front of the class and give a talk, but you could, Pat. Could you do it for me instead?" I was a little apprehensive but I knew all there was to know about St Bernadette and Lourdes, having read a lot of books on the subject and been there five times myself, so I agreed to do it.

It wasn't a Catholic school, but I found the students eager to learn all about it. I told them the story of a 14-year-old young girl, Bernadette Soubirous, from Lourdes, who in 1858 was very poor and suffered with asthma. Bernadette went out one day with her sister and a friend to collect firewood. Most of the wood lay on the other side of the river and her sister did not want Bernadette to wade across the cold waters, in case she caught a cold, as she would be coughing and wheezing all night with her asthma. Bernadette waited on the shore while the other two went across to get the wood.

I told the students that while Bernadette waited by herself on the river bank, a beautiful lady appeared, asking her to come back to that spot, and to say the rosary there, and that altogether she had 18 apparitions.

At that time in France, everyone had rosaries, especially the peasant children. Bernadette got hers out of her pocket and prayed the rosary. I told the children that unbeknown to Bernadette at the time, the beautiful lady who appeared was Mary, the Mother of Jesus, whom we Catholics call Our Blessed Lady. I told them about the miraculous spring that she helped Bernadette to find in the ground on one of her visits to the grotto that ran into a stream, which today has been converted into baths where people can bathe, with drinking taps installed, so people can drink the water and where some get cured of their illness. I finished my talk off by explaining how I was cured of cancer there years ago.

When I finally finished the talk the whole class had their hands up, bombarding me with questions. They also asked Ellen, who I had gone with, "Were you cured of your cancer there, and would you like to become a Catholic?"

"I don't know about that," she answered. "I think it's perhaps too late for me to change now."

"It's never too late," I piped up, but of course it never happened because shortly after that Ellen took a turn for the worse and died. She passed away very peacefully, with me saying the Divine Mercy prayer at her bedside in her home.

Another day at the hospital the priest asked us to go and see a man who kept having heart attacks. Father went on to say: "He really needs to go to Confession but won't hear of it. In fact, every time I go to see him, he tells me to get lost and swears at me, but do your best, you two. See what you can do. He just might open up to a woman."

I wondered what we would say to this man. His name was Tom, a big man with a beard.

"Hello Tom," we said, introducing ourselves. "We are

from the Catholic church. We help Father Anton visiting all the Catholics in this hospital, I understand that you are a Catholic?"

"Oh yes, but I gave all that up years ago."

"I see. Well what has been wrong with you Tom? What's brought you into hospital?"

"It's my heart. I keep having heart attacks."

"How many have you had?"

"Eight."

"Gosh, that's a lot, but you're on the mend again now, aren't you?"

"Yes."

"Well, aren't you a lucky man to have yet another chance to make your peace?"

"What do you mean?"

"Well I think God is trying to tell you something, and He's giving you chance after chance to come back to Him. He is knocking on the door of your heart Tom, but you won't let Him in. You see Jesus is so meek and humble at heart, and He won't impose on us unless we invite Him in." He seemed interested, so I went on: "Our souls govern our bodies, and when our soul is at peace, then it becomes easier for our bodies to heal and get stronger, because our emotions play a big part in our wellbeing. Just say, 'Jesus please help me', and He will. I am sure it will work. Would you like to accept a Miraculous Medal?" He did, and after putting one around his neck we left.

The following week, Father Anton said: "Pat, what on earth did you say to old Tom last week? I was on my rounds and popped my head around his curtain asking, 'Do you need me, my son?' That's when he said he'd like to go to Confession."

"Oh, that wasn't me, Father, that is the power of Our Lady's medal." He smiled. I must stress that I can't take any credit for anything that I did in the Legion because I was only an inferior tool in Her hands, as I was being used by God and guided by His Mother. You don't have to be clever or educated, just to go through the school of life, and the best school ever, Our Lady's school.

I used to get up every morning wondering where She would lead me that day, and what strangers I would meet who were Her earthly children that were in trouble or sick whom She wanted to help. They might be frightened and need a consoling word to cheer them and let them know that someone cares and will help them to carry their crosses. We all have crosses to bear from time to time, some more than others, but those crosses make us ready for heaven.

I remember going to a mission where every night a different priest came to talk on different subjects, and I'll never forget Father John Edwards who spoke about suffering. He recalled that at one of his Masses he had happened to say: "There is nothing that we cannot endure that Our Lord himself didn't suffer," and with that, one of his elderly parishioners shouted: "Oh yes there is Father. Jesus never grew old and didn't have arthritis like me." But this priest had a good answer for him. He said: "No, because Jesus was already pure enough and good enough for heaven. As we grow old and infirm we grow more humble, growing old puts us down a peg, making us nicer people. Suffering purifies the soul and makes us ready for heaven – I believe that." Father Edwards went on to say that Jesus did many wonderful things when He was on earth, curing people and performing miracles, but the most powerful thing He ever did was to redeem the world and He did that by being helpless on the cross. That was when He was most powerful, and likewise when we are sick or helpless we are imitating Jesus on the cross, especially if we offer it up to God: that is redemptive suffering.

There are two types of suffering that I have witnessed in the hospital. One sick person will moan and bewail their lot, talking about all the symptoms they have, some even become a pain in the neck with their moaning, but then there is the other type who never complains, accepts it all, and offers it up. They are more interested in others and what is going on around them, asking how things are going in the church or how is so-and-so, and by doing that they become special in God's eyes. You are closer to God during illness, because just as any good parent who is with a sick child becomes more concerned and loving towards that one more than the rest, so it is with Him. Never think that suffering is pointless or wasted. St Padre Pio used to say: "If we knew the value of suffering, we would surely ask for more." But it is human nature to shy away from pain and suffering. Even Our Lord on the Cross said: "Father, let this cup pass from me." Father Edwards said whenever he saw someone in a wheelchair, he saw a king on a throne.

One thing stuck in my mind that night and I felt that sermon was meant just for me, because at the time I was looking after my mother-in-law in a wheelchair and was finding it hard. He said: "Likewise, when you are looking after someone who is helpless and maybe confused, then you should be happy because you are sharing in the redemption." When he said that I felt ten feet tall; it changed my way of thinking and I thought, 'I will never moan again'. My attitude towards my mother-in-law and her suffering changed. I was inspired that night and after the Mass I went up to speak to that priest and thanked him. I think we should tell priests how much we appreciate their words because they need encouraging too, and they deserve praise when they inspire us; a good holy priest can save many souls.

I keep remembering the words Jesus said to His Apostles, (the first priests) when He sent them out to speak to the people: "Don't worry about what you will say because the words will be given to you. God's spirit will speak in your heart and just as the Father sent me, so I am sending you out to be my witnesses throughout the world." This is what I'm trying to do in this book, witnessing about His love that has touched my life so many times.

I read a story about what Jesus said to his Apostles about curing the sick: "You can do it too," He said, but they weren't sure that they could. St Andrew was the first one to cure someone (I think it was a blind man), and he came back to Jesus, excited telling him: "I've done it Lord, but how did I do it?"

Jesus said: "You did it three ways: first of all you had compassion for that man, secondly you did it in my name, and thirdly you believed." (And if you believe then you can move mountains).

Another story I read, which I decided to include in one of my recruitment drive speeches, was about Jesus' birth. As it was around Christmastime, I thought it appropriate. After the angel appeared to the shepherds, they set off to find the child in the stable and two of the shepherd boys decided to take a gift. The first one decided to take a lamb's fleece for baby Jesus to lie on, the second boy thought he would offer his packed lunch to Mary and Joseph to eat, but the third shepherd boy had nothing to give and was sad. On entering the stable, he went up to the baby in the manger and kissed his little feet. Whereupon Mary welcomed him with open arms saying: "Yours is the greatest gift of all because you have given us yourself." I concluded the talk with: "Likewise, by giving ourselves to God and His Blessed Mother, whether it be working in the Legion, or as a priest, or religious sister, then we are giving the best gift to God, and that is ourselves. Because the greatest gift we can give anyone is our self."

Home-to-Home

*I*t was a bitterly cold day and pouring with rain, when we were doing some home-to-home census work in another parish to find out how many Catholics lived there, so the register could be updated. I didn't relish walking the streets and knocking on doors in that weather. I would much rather be doing hospital work in the warm, but there are lots of different works in the Legion and we can't pick and choose. As it was a new Presidium, it was my job to show the members how it was done. When I arrived outside the church where I had arranged to meet my partner Ruth, I sat waiting for her in my car but after 15 minutes I thought, 'she's late.' I checked and realised it was me who was too early. I had arrived half an hour sooner then we had arranged, so with another 15 minutes to wait, I decided to use the time wisely and say the rosary, asking Our Lady to help us to be fruitful today. All sorts of negative thoughts were coming into my head like: 'What a rotten day to be outside.' I started to remonstrate with Her saying: "I will suffer for this later on with my arthritis. I am getting too old for this, after all, I am a grandmother of 12 now." I was seriously thinking of resigning from this branch, particularly as it was a spiritual desert in that area. No-one wanted to know about God any more I thought: it had been bad enough in my own parish, but even the priest at this parish was not interested in us. When I went to ask him if he would have the Legion in, he said that he would give it six months and if it didn't take off, it would have to close. Three people had joined, so with me helping that made two pairs working each week, and after existing for four months something had to happen soon to change his mind or we would have to close the branch down.

Tears started running down my face, I guess I was getting disheartened and worried about what would become of the group. We needed something uplifting to show the fruits of our labours – after all, it is the inspiring things that spur us on and nothing like that was happening where we were. Finally, Ruth my partner was in sight coming down the road with her umbrella up. I felt a tinge of shame complaining because she was in her 70s and had worse health problems than I did, yet she wasn't complaining.

One last little prayer before she reached the car: "Show me, dear Mother, one good reason why I shouldn't pack it all in." With that, I dried my eyes and quickly composed myself. Ruth got in the car and off we went to our first address. It was a very long road, which would take up all of our two hours, doing both sides. It was the same old story all along the road; no-one was interested in what we had to say. We explained that we were from the local Catholic church trying to find out how many Catholics live in the area, most said: "No, sorry," and closed the door; some didn't even open the door at all when they saw two ladies coming down the path, thinking we were canvassers selling something, or that we were Jehovah Witnesses. It was very disheartening. We did find one young man in a wheelchair who called us in and who was glad of the company, as he was housebound. He also happened to be a Catholic, but didn't go to Mass and we asked him if he would like to receive the sacraments because we could arrange a visit from the priest if he couldn't get to church because of his disabilities, and he said he would. We promised to arrange that.

As we were finishing canvassing in that road, and as our two hours were almost up, we knocked on the door of a house towards the end of the road. A young woman answered the door with a young baby in her arms and one-by-one, five other small children appeared, gathering around her feet. When we asked if there were any Catholics living there she said: "Yes, I am a Catholic but I haven't practised for years." I asked if she'd had the baby baptised yet: "No, in fact none of my six children have been christened." She went on to tell us that her mother, who had died recently and had been a devout Catholic, had always been encouraging her to get them 'done'.

"Perhaps she is still getting at me now through you, because you remind me of my mom," she said, after I had told her how important it was to baptise children and how at baptism we become part of God's family.

"Surely, as loving parents we want the ultimate best for our children that can be obtained for them, that being heaven one day, so why not have them all 'done'?" (as she had put it).

"Do you think I could have them all done at the same time, together?" she asked.

"I am sure that can be arranged," we reassured her. We told her we would have a word with the priest and get back to her.

We completed the road and decided to see the priest straight away. Ruth and I were elated all the way back to the church – just think, six little souls for God and a lapsed Catholic mother's promise to return to the faith. Our Lady had surely shown me not one, but seven good reasons not to pack it all in. She knew best and I was sorry for doubting Her. My views on home-to-home work changed considerably as I realised the value of it, for how else would we have found that family?

Our visit with the priest turned out to be very disappointing. He said: "It can't be done. How old are the children?"

"Between four months and 12 years Father."

"Well, the three youngest under seven may be able to be baptised in due course, after I see the parents attend Mass for twelve months, but the three older ones will have to come for instruction and may be ready in a year or so, but I can't promise anything. Go and tell the mother to come to Confession and attend Mass every week before I decide anything."

I was very upset about this, but went back to the family and explained what the priest had said. Carole, the mother, had a word with her husband, Trevor, who wasn't a Catholic and didn't know the rules of the church.

Trevor said: "It's all six together or none at all." We were sunk, we had lost them – or so we thought.

At the next meeting, we discussed the matter and decided to pray about it and leave it in Our Lady's hands, because if She wanted this, she would find a way. She surely did, and lost no time in sorting it out. Low and behold, a few days later, I got a phone call from one of the legionaries from that parish saying: "Pat, guess what! We are having a new priest next week."

"How come? What's happened to our present one?"

"He's been moved. Apparently, he was having a breakdown and has a drink problem. He was taken away last night and admitted into a clinic, poor man."

"That explains a lot," I said. "I guess he was having a job coping with his regular work, without us adding to his burden. Let's see what the new priest has to say about it. We will ask him."

At the following meeting, who should be in attendance but the new parish priest whom I recognised from another parish? I knew he was a priest in favour of the Legion and had a great love for Our Lady. When we explained our dilemma, and that the parents wanted all their six children baptised together, he said: "I don't see why not. Tell the family I will call to see them this week to arrange it." My heart leapt. Thank you, Blessed Mother. She knew the first priest couldn't do it and She found one who could. I had sensed an urgency to see this through, and judging by how quickly it was all happening now, I think She did too.

We visited Carole, who told us it had all been arranged

for the next Sunday morning, but she needed Godparents for the children – and would we do the honours? I was with a different partner that day and we decided to take two children each, with Ruth, my first partner, taking the other two; so we were their Godmothers. It was all happening so quickly, it was uncanny.

It was a lovely day that Sunday. We were all in church, and after the six Baptisms we took some photos on the altar, and then there was a lovely party at the family's home; a joyous occasion and one to thank God for. Carole and Trevor, the parents, were very happy, especially when us Legionaries presented them with two large framed pictures of the Sacred Hearts of Jesus and Mary to commemorate the day. These pictures took pride of place on the wall of their lounge. I remembered as a child how two similar pictures at my grandmother's house influenced my life; I wouldn't be without the Sacred Heart in my home.

With this turn of events, the Legion members were on a high for a while, but seven days later the joy turned to sadness when the children's daddy, Trevor, was killed in an explosion. He had been a car mechanic by trade, and at weekends he used to repair cars at home in his garage to earn extra cash. On this particular morning Trevor was using a portable gas heater in the garage, as it was very cold. He was fixing a blockage in the fuel pipe of the car and as he blew down the fuel pipe to unblock it, he spilt petrol on to the flame of the heater and the heater exploded. This first explosion caused the petrol tank of the car to explode, blowing the whole garage up, with Trevor in it. He was 33 years old when he died. His eldest daughter was playing in the street when it happened and heard her daddy screaming: "God help me!"

When I heard the news, I drove over to comfort Carole who was left with six young children; it was the worst tragedy I had ever heard of. Everyone was in shock and disbelief.

At Trevor's funeral the following week, the same priest who had performed the Baptisms of the children, performed the funeral. After the internment at the cemetery, I spoke to the priest saying that I couldn't help feeling that there had been a Divine Intervention happening over the past few weeks leading up to this. I felt God knew what was going to happen to Trevor, and had seen to it that his children were Baptised first, and he agreed with me. Later, I also realised that the other priest who was now in a clinic, would not have been able to cope with this tragedy in the same way this priest coped, being such a great support to the family. Sadly though, later that year, this same priest was found dead at the wheel of his car having suffered a heart attack. He was only 42.

Carole told me that Trevor had told her that he wanted to become a Catholic on the morning of his death. As he was looking at the two holy pictures on the wall he said; "Will you see that priest for me and ask him what I have to do?" I told Carole, not to worry, because God knew what was in his heart and would have accepted him as such; there is such a thing as baptism of desire.

We kept in touch with the family for a couple of years. Carole seemed to be coping so well: she learnt to drive, bought a large caravan and took the children to the seaside on holiday. I told her I was so proud of her; what she was doing on her own with all those children was wonderful. She seemed to get such strength from up above. The last I heard was that she had met a soldier who wanted to marry her and take on the children. I was so pleased for her; she deserved some happiness after all she'd been through. Eventually I lost touch with her as I left that praesidium.

A year or so later, back at my own branch of the legion, I was asked to visit a family whose son had committed suicide. I knew from experience what the family was going through, having lost my brother, Frank in the same way. I told them about Frank; the lad's mother told me that her son was depressed after splitting up with his girlfriend and had driven his car down a country lane, parked up and gassed himself in his car. It was too late by the time the police found him. I remembered the words that the priest had said to me when Frank died, and I repeated them to her. I told her to pray for him and have some Masses said for him and that I would remember them all in my prayers. The loss of a child is the worst possible thing that can happen to you, and it is something that you never get over, as I was to find out in the future, when I lost my daughter.

Caroline

My daughter Caroline suffered with asthma. It developed when she was in her teens: our cat set her off and we found that she was allergic to animals, dogs as well as cats. She got married young and had had four children by the time she and her husband split up. Her asthma got steadily worse, with the stress of being on her own with young children and trying to hold down two part-time jobs to make ends meet. Eighteen months before her fatal attack she had a near-fatal attack and two heart attacks in the ambulance that weakened her heart, and as a consequence she did not recover after her next bad attack.

I was with her the time before. She came to our house on the way home from the doctor's with asthma. The doctor had put her on a nebuliser and she seemed a lot better in the surgery, but on the way home she stopped her car outside our house and collapsed inside our front door. I called the ambulance, which arrived in no time as the ambulance station is just up the road, but her airways had cut off and she was unconscious. The paramedics gave her an injection to open her airways then put her in the ambulance. The monitors that she was wired up to suddenly went dead, and I couldn't understand why the ambulance wasn't moving and rushing her to hospital, but they were waiting for the drug they had administered to kick in and bring her back to life. I was praying out loud. I put a medal in her hand and pleaded with God to give her back to us. Her body suddenly jerked, she gasped for air and she was back with us, then it was full speed ahead to the hospital, in and out of traffic with the sirens going to get there quickly.

When we arrived at the hospital the paramedics told the

doctors that Caroline had 'arrested' twice and they thought they had lost her. Even though she came back round, it was still grave and she was sent to the intensive care unit, with a team of doctors and nurses attending to her. I tried to contact Father Anton at the hospital, but it was his afternoon off. He was shopping in the city when I got him on his mobile.

"Is it serious, Pat?"

"Yes, Father."

"Then I'm on my way in a taxi. I'll be there in ten minutes." True to his word, bless him, he arrived and anointed Caroline. She pulled through that time, but the next time she wasn't so lucky and I couldn't be with her in her last moments.

I wrote to the ambulance depot thanking the young man for saving my daughter's life that day, because he was really wonderful and wouldn't give up on her. He had kept persevering with her, but as well as his medical expertise at work that day, my prayers and faith were also at work. In my letter I told him that she was now back at home with her four children, who were very grateful to have their mummy back. I later heard that that young paramedic who saved her life was awarded a medal for saving the most lives that year. I learnt this from my nephew who was also in the ambulance service at the time. I really feel that the Divine Mercy prayer was instrumental in helping that man to bring Caroline back to life. Do not tell me that prayers don't work, especially when you pray with conviction and belief.

Eighteen months later, Caroline suffered her final attack. I couldn't be with her. I saw her at five o'clock in the evening when she came to pick up John-Paul, who was going to the pictures with her son Lee and she was giving them both a lift. It was Saturday night and she was fine then. I told her that I was off to Dublin on the eight o'clock plane that evening and would see her on Monday. She said she would meet me off the plane, to save me getting a taxi home. "Good," I said, "I'd rather give you some petrol money instead." But of course that never happened: it was the last time I ever saw her. Caroline went out with some friends for a drink that evening, and afterwards went back to a friend's house where there was a longhaired dog. It affected her breathing immediately. Her friends opened the windows to give her some air and fetched her inhaler from her car but it didn't help, so they phoned for an ambulance, which incidentally took 21 minutes to arrive. By this time she was outside on the front lawn, unconscious. She was pronounced dead on arrival at the hospital.

The next morning, the police woke my husband up. They were standing at the door with Lee, Caroline's eldest son, and took them to identify her body in the hospital morgue. That was a terrible ordeal for them, and of course I was away in Dublin and didn't know what had happened. Before he phoned me to break the sad news, I had a premonition that something was terribly wrong: it was so strange, I couldn't shake it off, and I want to share it with you.

I had arrived in Dublin on Saturday evening and went straight to bed in the guesthouse. I fell asleep quickly but woke up at about two o'clock in the morning with a terrible feeling of dread in my stomach, I realise now that it must have been the precise moment that my daughter had passed away. I believe every mother senses when her child is in trouble.

Even before I caught the plane in Birmingham, I had wanted to turn back. I had been asked to go to the information desk over the tannoy, which was strange because when I got there they said it was a mistake. They thought I had left my handbag behind but my bag was on my shoulder and it wasn't mine. Everything was like a dream. I felt I shouldn't be going and wanted to turn back. On the plane, I started to say the rosary, as I often did on flights, praying for a safe journey, but for some reason I offered my rosary up for all those who were to die that night, never dreaming that one of them would be my beautiful girl.

On Sunday morning I had woken up still with this foreboding feeling but didn't know why. After breakfast I made my way into town by bus to the Concillium, the legion headquarters, but as I had arrived an hour too early, I decided that I wouldn't go into the meeting room just yet. There are lots of beautiful churches in Dublin, one being Our Lady and the Angel's church, which was only a few yards away from where I was, in the same road. I could see the church, with ornate statues of angels all around the building; it was the same church that our founder Frank Duff used every day. I had never been in there before so I walked up to this church, but the gates were locked and I couldn't get in. I stood there looking through the iron railings and realised that the church must be being refurbished because there were lots of old benches and rubble outside. Right in front of me, behind the railings, was a life-size statue of the crucifixion, with Jesus on the cross and Our Lady, His Mother, on one side and St John on the other side of Him. It looked a terribly sad scene to me, especially with all the bricks and rubble piled up around it; a bit like a bombsite or war zone.

A strange feeling came over me and I wanted to cry. I looked at the statue of the Mother of Sorrows, with Her head bowed down, wearing a wavy veil, and I felt weak all of a sudden as if I was going to faint. I grabbed the bars saying: "What is it? What are you trying to tell me? What is wrong?" Looking back now, I realise that She wasn't the only Mother of Sorrows then. I walked away from that sad scene holding the walls to help me stand up, and was glad to sit down in Demontfort House before making myself a cup of tea in the kitchen. I was still drinking that tea, getting over my strange experience, when one of the Dublin legionaries came to tell me I was wanted on the telephone; it was my husband calling to tell me the devastating news. I was in a daze; nothing was real. When my colleagues learned the news they were rallying round making me cups of tea and trying to get me on the first flight home.

The next available flight was at 8pm that evening, so I had to wait six hours in turmoil. That was the longest day of my life. When I got home to Birmingham Airport, the whole family were there to meet me. I thought, 'Pat, you have got to be brave for their sakes.' Seeing how devastated they all were, I felt I could not fall apart. Our David kissed me and said: "We're glad you're home, mom, because you're the strong one, stronger than us." Inside I was broken-hearted, I was like a soldier who is badly wounded but has to carry on the battle. Yes, the loss of a child is too much to bear and the worst thing that can happen in life. Roy was more broken-hearted than I was. He idolised our Caroline, they were very close and he was a broken man.

The next day, I watched him through the kitchen window, sitting in the garden. Being July, it was a warm sunny day. I prayed for him, asking the Holy Spirit, (The Comforter), to come down on him with His healing power. When he came back indoors he said he felt something touch him out there and believed it was Caroline giving him a hug. It was so sad. You don't think you will get through something like that but good friends and family were there for us, and the little old Irish priest from our church at the time was a great support, calling in nearly every day.

The church was packed for Caroline's funeral. She had lots of friends and was greatly loved. She was beautiful inside as well as on the outside, looking like a model. We were so proud of her, the way she turned heads wherever she went. Six priests were on the altar: Father Anton from the hospital, the two missionary priests who were friends of the family, and three other priests that I knew from the Legion, and most of my Legion colleagues were there too. Eighty-three

Mass cards were collected that day, so I was sure that she would be in Heaven with all those Masses being said for her. We hired the church hall for refreshments afterwards and I was amazed at all the help that friends provided, without asking. It was such a support to us.

I remember reading that in China when a child or young person dies there is a great celebration in the streets because they believe that that person has found favour with God and has been spared old age, as their soul is ready for and worthy of heaven now. All I know is that death is definitely not the end. This life is just a waiting time, to get to where we are destined and we shouldn't waste a minute of it because once gone, no part of our life can ever be recaptured and we don't get a second chance. We have one continuous life but in two parts, one on earth and the other in eternity.

I was given this beautiful poem called A Letter From Heaven, which was very comforting to me and it's just what I believe our departed loved ones would say to us. Since then, I have photocopied it hundreds of times and given it to bereaved families. I have even used it at funerals as a eulogy; I think it is beautiful. Here is the poem:

A Letter From Heaven

To my dearest family, some things I'd like to say,
But first of all to let you know, I arrived OK.
I'm writing this from heaven where I dwell with God above,
Where there's no more tears or sadness, there is just eternal love.
Please do not be unhappy just because I'm out of sight,
Remember that I'm with you, every morning noon and night.
That day I had to leave you when life on earth was through,
God picked me up and hugged me and he said, "I welcome you.
It's good to have you back again; you were missed when you were gone,
And as for your dearest family, they will be here later on.
I need you here so badly as part of my big plan,
There's so much we have to do here to help our mortal man."
Then God gave me a list of things he wished for me to do

And foremost on that list of mine is to watch and care for you.
And I will be besides you every day week and year,
And when you're sad I am standing there to wipe away the tear.
When you lie in bed at night the days chores put to flight,
God and I are closer to you in the middle of the night.
When you think of my life on earth, and all those living years,
Because your only human, they are bound to bring you tears.
But do not be afraid to cry, it does relieve the pain,
Remember there would be no flowers unless there were some rain.
I wish that I could tell you all that God has planned,
But if I were to tell, you wouldn't understand.
But one thing is for certain though my life on earth's no more;
I am closer to you now than I ever was before.
And to my many friends, trust God knows what is best,
I'm still not very far from you, I'm just beyond the crest.
There are rocky roads ahead of you and many hills to climb,
But together we can do it, taking one step at a time.
It was always my philosophy and I would like it for you too,
That as you give unto the world, so the world will give to you.
If you can help somebody who's in sorrow or in pain,
Then you can say to God at night my day was not in vain.
And now I am contented that my life was worthwhile,
Knowing that as I passed along the way I made somebody smile.
So if you meet somebody who is down or feeling low,
Just lend a hand to pick them up as on your way you go.
When you are walking down the street and you have got me on your mind,
I am walking in your footstep only half a step behind.
And when you feel a gentle breeze or the wind upon your face,
That's me giving you a great big hug or just a soft embrace.
And when it's time for you to go from that body to be free,
Remember, you're not going, you're coming here to me.
And I will always love you from that land way up above, will be in touch soon.

PS: God sends his love.

Living with Grief

*I*n our Legion handbook, it says that as Legionaries we must be prepared to accept not only the joys but also the sorrows of Our Lady. It was time for me to experience one of Her greatest sorrows and to find out how She felt at the loss of Her Son. My daughter was tired and Jesus rescued her and took her to Himself and I must accept His will. God alone can see the future and maybe He was sparing her a life of worse suffering. When I visit anyone with emphysema or lung cancer, fighting for their breath, or an invalid on oxygen in a wheelchair, I'd wonder if that's what Caroline would have ended up like if she had lived, and whether I could have borne seeing her like that. I don't know which would be worst, the shock of losing her so suddenly or watching her with a prolonged illness, where I would feel so helpless. I think, given the choice, I would say: "Take her now, Lord."

But what about her four children? That was my first thought when I heard the news. What is going to become of them? The three younger children was now staying with their father and his partner who had two children the same ages and they could play together. Caroline's children had got to know them over the past two years as they stayed with their father sometimes at weekends, the oldest Lee, was staying with us. Lauren, the youngest, was 5 years old; Mitchell 7; Aleshia 13, and the oldest, Lee, was 16 when Caroline died.

A year later I was told that their dad and his partner were selling up and moving to Spain to live, taking all the children with them. I was upset at losing them as well as their mom, but Father Kemp our parish priest and a good friend said: "It is best if they go with their dad as it will give you time to come to terms with your grief." Not long after going to

Spain, the children came to visit and stayed for a few weeks. After a few months in Spain the eldest girl Aleshia came back asking if she could live with us.

While in Spain for seven years, the children came back three or four times a year for a holiday with us: every Christmas, Easter and in the school summer holidays for six weeks and we also went over to Spain every year to visit them. We used to hire a villa with a swimming pool and have the children come and stay there with us. They really looked forward to that. Their stepbrother and sister came too.

They were living in a little village in the desert, called Velez Rubio, with nothing much for the children to do, and they did get bored. The town was named after St Jose Maria Rubio, whom Pope John Paul had canonised a few years before. I used to pray to that Saint to look after the children for me while they were there. Their father had gone there because there was lots of building work going on and that was his line of work. It wasn't long before all the children could speak fluent Spanish; I was so proud of how they were coping. Their stepmother was good to them – it was a lot for her, taking on four more children as well as her own two.

We took them clothes and whatever they needed. We wouldn't have been able to afford to do that if it wasn't for my mother, their great grandmother, giving me money for them. My good sister Carole, who was now living in Germany, used to treat them sending money over; they wanted for nothing, except their lovely mother. I remember one day just after Caroline had died going down to her house and hearing the children playing in the back garden. I opened the back gate to see little Lauren, aged 5, riding her bike round and round in circles saying over and over again: "I want my mommy, I want my mommy." I ran over to her and hugged her and cried. Their dad and Michelle, his partner, were there clearing the house and all Caroline's possessions were in a heap in the back garden. That upset me because there was stuff in there that I would have liked, but they never thought to ask me. They moved back into that house for a few months before moving to Spain, getting it ready to let out when they had gone. When I visited I'd think 'this is my daughter's house, these are my grandchildren but this isn't my daughter'. It was weird.

Around Christmas time I decided to take the children to a pantomime. I went to buy the tickets and was just coming out of the booking office and getting into my car when a young woman, who looked like Caroline passed by and gave me such a loving smile that I thought it was her coming to say, "Thanks, mom, for what your doing for the children." I opened the car door and stood there watching her walk past. She walked with the same bounce that Caroline had and I sat in the car sobbing for ages before I could drive off.

I understand there are different stages of grief. Firstly, it is shock and disbelief, and then you get angry and ask, 'why? And, because you have that person on your mind all the time, you think you see them and it is quite natural. Many times I have sensed Caroline's presence near me, when her daughter Aleshia came to live with us for eight years it was like having Caroline back – we even made the mistake of calling her Caroline many times because she looked just like her mom, especially when she grew her hair long and dyed it blonde like her mom's.

Grief is just like an illness: you have to ease up and rest to recover, but I was doing the opposite. I was trying to keep extra busy because sitting in the house was making me morose, so I went out as much as I could. Consequently I became very tired and confused. Sometimes, while driving I'd have to think, 'where am I going?' and in the supermarket once, I walked off with someone else's trolley by mistake. One Sunday I went to church with odd shoes on – I have two pairs of navy blue shoes, almost identical, but one pair had higher heels than the other. I never noticed they were odd until I clip-clopped up the aisle to Holy Communion. Silly me. Yes, with grief comes confusion and it is all, 'If only'. I wish I had done that, I wish I had said that. Roy said: "I never did mend that leaking tap for her. Too late now." Simple things like that can make you feel guilty, so now I never put off till tomorrow what I can do today, because who knows – I may not have tomorrow.

We have Caroline's photo on the mantelpiece in our lounge and I talk to her every day and often visit her grave too. Next to where she is buried is a grave of another young woman who died the same week as my daughter, at 24 years old after having her tonsils out and haemorrhaging later. Her poor mother has been at her grave every single day grieving for the past eleven years. I can bet that whatever day I go to the cemetery she is there, sitting on a bench that has her daughter's nameplate on it, in her memory. Her grave is a shrine, with candles burning day and night and masses of flowers. I sit with that mother and tell her she has got to let go like I have, but even now she cannot get on with her life and finds it difficult. I am too busy getting on with life, because life is precious and shouldn't be wasted.

I read a lot and came across this book called *Embracing the Light*, by Jean Eddie, who haemorrhaged and died, also after an operation, but was brought back to life when the nursing staff found her half-an-hour later. She says in the book that she didn't want to come back after her experience of life after death. She said: "God embraces us and welcomes us regardless of our sins because he is pure love." She describes Heaven how I have always imagined it. We know our sins and that we are not worthy to be in God's presence, so we gladly go to be made worthy and pure in his sight. The way she described everything there was so incredibly beautiful.

A friend of Caroline's came to see me 12 months after she died and said she worked for the Asthma Association and had raised money through sponsors to enable me to get her a headstone for her grave. I was wondering how I was going to get one. We put some money towards what she gave me and we bought a nice big stone, with a statue of Our Lady on it and had it erected on her grave. Yes, Caroline is helping me from above and providing for her children too.

Saint Faustina, who had visions of Jesus, lost her best friend one day and asked Jesus: "Why did God take that mother away from her four young children, leaving them orphans? Wasn't that cruel?"

Jesus said: "Don't you know that that mother will be able to do much more for her children from heaven than ever she could on earth?" If you saw how Caroline's children were provided for, how they grew up unscathed and happy, you would believe that. I do. They are all grown up now: the eldest, Lee, has two children of his own and Aleshia is expecting her first baby, so Caroline would be a grandmother had she lived. Mark and David are both grandparents now too and so we are blessed with four great-grandchildren, and another on the way.

Pilgrimages

One person that my friend, Sister Maureen the nun, introduced me to was a lovely lady called Joan. When I first met her she was suffering with breast cancer and we became life-long friends. She recovered from the cancer, only to go on suffering with one illness after another. Since I have known her she has had eight strokes, each one leaving her more disabled, with heart failure and Chronic Obstructive Pulmonary Disease (COPD or emphysema) among other complaints. I've never known anyone suffer so much. Joan is a widow who lives by herself; she never complains and is one of those redemptive sufferers that I mentioned, who sits saying the rosary every day. She is so precious to God that whatever she asks for in her prayers, He grants. So if I need a special favour I ask Joan to pray for me and she comes up trumps every time. Talk about miracles on tap, she is overflowing with them.

Joan has taught me so much about suffering and what a beautiful person she is through it. I'm afraid I could never be so brave and would have given up long ago, but instead she baffles the doctors, going in and out of intensive care in hospital and rallying round, to their amazement. Time and time again her family have been sent for because she was at death's door, like when her windpipe collapsed and she had to have a false one fitted with a stent in, only to be saved again. She has been ill, non-stop for 30 years, but I am convinced she is still here for a purpose and her time is not yet up.

Three years ago we went to Lourdes together. Joan was in a wheelchair and I had recently had a knee replacement and found it difficult pushing her around, but we had a wonderful week. Joan was in raptures at it all; like a little child in Disney World. We got priority treatment everywhere we went – we didn't have to wait in queues because wheelchairs are allowed to go straight to the front – and I got help up hills from fellow pilgrims to push Joan's chair. We managed to visit all the places of interest, and Our Lady was with us all the way.

As well as pilgrimages to Lourdes, I loved going to Medjugorje where there have been daily apparitions since 1981. Before going there I thought there never would be anywhere like Lourdes, but Medjugorje was something else. It was there that I first experienced passing out with the Spirit after the laying-on-of-hands by a priest called Father Yozo; he was the priest who helped the children when they first started seeing Our Lady; a very holy man. Everyone was going up to the altar to be blessed by Father Yozo, falling down like flies, passing out in ecstasy. I was rather nervous of falling back, even though someone was there to catch me, and at first I swayed and was fighting it, but the priest persevered with me and I suddenly realised that I must not reject the Holy Spirit. In an instant I said within myself: 'Come Holy Spirit, Come,' inviting Him in, whereupon I felt a surge that knocked me off my feet and back onto to the floor. I lay there for what seemed like ages drinking in the wonderful feeling of love, just as if Our Lord had embraced me. I can only describe it as the thrill of a first kiss of a young girl in love.

I got up and went back to my seat in church and broke down and cried. If ever I had doubted God before I never will again, because He had touched me that day. That was where I learnt that Jesus is so meek and humble – He will not impose Himself on us unless we invite Him in. I have been back to that place three times in groups of 20 or more; it became my spiritual fix for the year. Speak to anyone who has been there, and they will tell you the same.

We climbed the rugged hill of the apparitions and sat on the top of the mountain overlooking the peaceful town. The villagers there are lovely people who can't do enough for you and we stayed in their farmhouses. I shared a bedroom with my two friends. Sister Maureen and Mary Brown, an invalid lady in a wheelchair. She was born with cerebral palsy and didn't walk but came on all the pilgrimages. She was so devout and was the best company in the entire world. They were the happiest weeks being in such wonderful company like that: I really have walked amongst saints.

Our return flight was delayed and we were given a complimentary bottle of wine each to compensate for our wait. Mary and I had a fit of the giggles on the plane after drinking it and you could say that we were high in the sky in more ways than one; even Sister Maureen sitting next to us could hardly contain herself, especially when I asked Mary what was she going to do with all those empty statues of Our Lady Queen of Peace. Unlike at Lourdes, there was no spring of Holy Water to fill them with where we had been. She replied: "Well, I have some Lourdes water at home, also some water from Holywell and I'll mix them altogether and people will then have the three shrines in one!" We all burst out laughing; she was so comical with her Geordie accent and wonderful dry sense of humour.

We were going back there the following year but we didn't have a spiritual director to go with us – the two priests that I had already asked couldn't come because of other commitments that week elsewhere. I happened to be at Mass in Sister Maureen's parish and noticed a priest I had never met before, kneeling down in church after Mass and was drawn to turn back and speak to him. I asked him if he had ever been to Medjugorje and he said, "No", then I said: "Would you like to go, Father, because I have a free seat on our trip and we can't get a priest to accompany the group?" His face lit up and he said: "Yes, I would." And so it was that he came with us that year and thoroughly enjoyed it. On the way back home on the plane he came and sat with me, as I had an empty seat next to me and he said how much he had enjoyed the week and how grateful he was that I had asked him, because he wouldn't have missed it for the world. He was curious as to why I had chosen him to go. I told him that it seemed the right thing to do as I was drawn to him, and maybe Our Lady wanted it. "Well," he said. "I am so glad you did, and I think you're right." Strange as it may seem, what I did not know was that this priest was dying, so I believe Our Lady wanted to show him a bit of Heaven before he went for his reward soon afterwards. You might say I look too deeply into things, but I don't think these happenings were coincidental.

Business Problems

*I*n the 1980s there was a recession in England and thousands of businesses were 'folding up' and 'going to the wall', including my husband's business. He had tried to keep it going for as long as he could, borrowing money from the bank to keep the business afloat and keep the men in work, but some of the small firms that he had supplied windows to went bust, owing him thousands of pounds, and he was slowly going bankrupt himself. Apart from that, his factory unit had been burgled six times in one year and the insurers refused to pay out, due to a technicality. The last time the unit was burgled, all the office equipment and tools were stolen but because they had been moved to a different, more secure room than the one stated on the policy, the insurance company refused to pay out.

It seemed that every month he would come home on a Monday to say that over the weekend he had been burgled and he just couldn't afford to replace the equipment; it was a terrible struggle for him. I decided to ask my best friend to help and thought, 'I know what I will do.' I had a framed picture of the Immaculate Heart of Mary and took it down to the factory and hung it up on the wall of the office, consecrating the unit to Our Lady, asking Her to look after the place for me, and to stop all these break-ins. I left Her to do just that, but the very next week Roy informed me that thieves got in again last night. "Oh no," I said, "I trusted in Our Lady to stop all that. Why hasn't She done what I asked?"

"Wait," said Roy. "You haven't heard the rest of it yet. The burglars got in through a 2ft wide skylight on the roof, unbolted all the equipment, putting it all on stacker-trucks to wheel out of the roller-shutter doors, which are operated from inside the building. The idea was to load it all into vans parked outside. However, they didn't get away with a thing. The roller-shutter doors jammed after opening a couple of inches and the burglars couldn't get the gear out. They had to leave empty-handed the same way they got in." I wonder who had done that?

Roy had to close the business in the end and was eventually put in a dangerous position when the bank threatened to repossess our home. We had managed to get a mortgage when things were better, but it looked like we were going to lose our home if something didn't happen soon.

Instead of bankruptcy, Roy went into a voluntary arrangement with the bank to pay back every penny that he owed, trying to be honourable. With high interest rates, it was crippling us. Reading a Sacred Heart messenger book, I noticed an advertisement for a house to let in Fatima, Portugal. It was suitable for religious groups to stay while on pilgrimage there. I thought it would be nice for the legionaries to go sometime later on when we could afford it, so I phoned the owner asking if the house was suitable for a wheelchair, as we couldn't go without Mary Brown. She said there were no steps up to the house and thought it would be all right, but why didn't I go over myself to check it out first?, as it was empty the following week.

"How much do you charge?" I asked.

"Nothing," came the reply. "Just put some money in the meter for the amount of electricity that you use. All you will need is your airfare, which is about a hundred pounds." We could manage that. Apparently, it was her holiday home that she didn't use much since her husband had died, so Roy, John-Paul and I went to Portugal and visited Fatima nearly every day.

It was a nice big house, with plenty of bedrooms and a chapel in one of the downstairs rooms, but it was about 20 miles from the shrine in Fatima and would involve too much driving for the group of legionaries. We would have to hire a mini-bus, one that was adapted for Mary's wheelchair and with no-one else who was a driver in the group, apart from me, I deemed it unsuitable and I definitely couldn't see myself driving on the other side of the road like Roy was. We would have to look out for somewhere nearer to the shrine if we wanted to take a trip there in future. Otherwise, it was great: set in a pine forest, and near a lagoon that you could swim in.

It was a real blessing that we were able to go and spend a week there, and I'm so glad that we did. It was strange how I found that advertisement, but there was something else remarkable about that house and its owner. It wasn't until the day we were leaving that we found out who the owner was. On that day two priests, who had booked the house for the following week, arrived. They asked us if we knew who owned the house. I said: "Mrs Theodore Gregson."

"Yes, John Gregson the film star; Theodore is his widow." We had been staying in a film star's home and didn't know. There was a story in one of the books in that house, written by John Gregson, about his experience up the mountain in Medjugorje, on a pilgrimage that he made just before his death a few years ago and how he loved that place. I've always liked him as a film star ever since he starred in *Genevieve*, but had never connected the name in the short story to him.

While we were in the house, Roy found some fishing gear and decided to take John-Paul fishing in the lagoon. They came back with nothing. While they were away, I sat reading the visitors' comments and decided to include my own, and on a few extra pieces of paper I wrote a short story to put in the visitors book. It was mainly about how much I loved Our Lady and how I had come on this pilgrimage to ask Her help with our situation back home. I also wrote about my cure at Lourdes and how I joined the Legion of Mary to repay Her for Her kindness.

A couple of weeks later, I got a letter from one of the priests who stayed in the house after us, saying that he had got my address off Mrs Gregson so that he could write and thank me for such an inspiring story that I had left in the visitors book. Another letter arrived after that, from a nun who also had stayed in the house, saying what a wonderful story I had written in the house. These letters made me think that perhaps one day, when I had the time, I could write a book, and I guess that time is now.

Until recently, all my leisure time was taken up with knitting for the grandchildren, or crocheting blankets for friends and family, there was always someone having a baby or some old person who would be glad of a shawl or knee-blanket in the winter. I also made some for the church building-fund to be sold in aid of the church roof repairs. I had filled my time knitting and crocheting but recently I developed a cough which lasted for a year and was diagnosed with asthma; the wool fibres were affecting my chest, so I had to give it up. With time on my hands, and not being a person who can sit doing nothing, I found myself writing this book.

Another strange thing had happened to me in Fatima. We wanted to visit the convent where Sister Lucia, one of the children who saw Our Lady, now lived. We travelled along the coast to Coimbra, hoping to catch a glimpse of her, but when we got there we were told that wasn't possible, as she didn't make appearances. We were very disappointed. We did however go inside the convent front door and bought some pictures of the life-size statues of the Sacred Hearts that were on each side of the door.

On our way back we stopped at a place called Nazaire, and had a picnic on the beach; it was October but still very warm. I noticed a little old church opposite and decided to walk across and take a look inside; it looked just like the churches in the western films in Mexico, with a bell hanging above the doorway. Leaving Roy and John-Paul on the beach, I walked inside. It was very dark inside but on one side of the altar was a large statue of Our Lady of Fatima, a very early one, almost eighty years old, it was greyish-white alabaster, very pale. As I looked at it I realised that something wasn't quite right: instead of Our Lady's hands being clasped in prayer, or Her arms outstretched as in other Fatima statues, this one had one hand hanging down and the other arm bent at the elbow and wrist, with Her hand turned round in a 'stop' position, just like a policeman holding up his hand to stop the traffic. My first reaction was that some naughty person had bent the arm into that position, as the arms were jointed at the elbow and wrist, but no. I sensed something strange; I was mesmerised. I sensed She was trying to tell me something, She knew that I was very worried and distressed about the possibility of losing our home and was telling me to stop worrying, for everything was going to be all right. I sat there for a while, then left the church and went outside to fetch Roy to come and take a look and tell me what he thought of it. He didn't get the chance though, because out of nowhere came a big black Labrador dog foaming at the mouth. It started attacking us, biting our heels and making John-Paul scream. I was hitting the dog with a towel but he was biting holes in it and frightening us. John-Paul's bare feet were bleeding, so we all made a run for it to the car, parked nearby leaving the dog chewing on John-Paul's shoes that he had left behind. Being the same shoe-size as myself at the time, John-Paul had to wear a spare pair of my pumps for the rest of the journey.

Another place we visited in Portugal that time was Figueira Da Foz, where we went to a marketplace and a fish market that had live crabs walking about across the floor and under your feet; we had to step over them. One of the stalls had statues of Our Lady of Fatima for sale and I bent down to look closely at them. I had looked at many of those statues all over Fatima and the surrounding places, but didn't buy one because none of the faces did Her justice. They had beady eyes and some were even cross-eyed, but here, I noticed this one was just right. The face was smiling gently and was so beautiful that I bought it. The old peasant lady was so happy to make a sale she hugged me; I think she needed the money. In broken English she told me that if I took this statue home with me I would have many blessings, and I have.

When we arrived home, I read that when you see a pale-looking statue like the one I had seen in that church, it was a sign that She was concerned about one of Her children. This was so strange because I'd prayed to Her to help us with our financial difficulties and She certainly did.

A month or so after our trip my neighbour and friend, Blanche died, leaving me a substantial amount of money in her will. Her husband Owen had passed away before her and she had had to go into a nursing home. I had to sell her home for her to pay the exorbitant fees for the care home but she still had a fair amount in the bank, which was left to me, having no family of her own. We were able to pay our debts at the bank and save our home. I treated all the family and paid my sister Carole back the money she had given me to get to Lourdes, with interest. A lot of good was done with that money; I helped a lot of people and didn't waste a penny of it. I often go to visit the grave of Blanche and Owen and say a prayer for them, and thank them for the money they left us that changed our lives.

My mother looked at me one day and said: "Who would have believed it, Pat? That Pat Murray, that poor little girl who didn't have a Communion dress, would end up a woman of substance as you have become? But I tell you love, if you do God's work, you get God's pay and you'll never want." That is true.

Sometimes, mom would make a lot of sense, but other times, she talked a lot of nonsense and I despaired of her.

She didn't like me flying on planes because she was terrified of flying herself. I could never get her to come to Lourdes with me because of that. She tried to stop me from going to Dublin, especially when the IRA was active and threatening to blow up planes. She would say: "You're chancing your luck, my girl. One of these days there will be a bomb on that plane, and you will be blown up. You mustn't go." But of course I did.

One time on my way to Dublin, I arrived at Birmingham Airport to find soldiers with guns, all over the place. They had been put on bomb alert and it had been on the news. I was going through the barrier with my hand luggage, just an overnight bag and my handbag, when I was stopped and called over to the desk because of something suspicious in my handbag. What was it? I couldn't think and told them: "I don't know what you mean." Then in a serious tone they said: "There is something metal, it is only small." I still couldn't think what it could be, then suddenly it dawned on me that it was my miraculous medals that I always carry with me: a little bundle of about 20 medals, and they think it's a bomb.

"Oh, I know what it is," I smiled. It's my medals."

"Medals, what kind of medals? Good conduct medals from the IRA?"

"No," I laughed. "Like this gold one around my neck, only they are smaller and silver coloured. Here, I'll show you," and tried to open my bag, but was stopped in my tracks.

"Don't touch the bag madam." They were very serious and as I looked behind me, I saw a soldier pointing a gun my way. I thought, 'Oh dear, I'm going to be marched into a room now and searched. I might even miss my plane. Why does everything happen to me? If my mother could see me now she would have a heart attack.' One of the officials, a young Irish man said: "Just a minute. Miraculous medals? I know about them, I'm a Catholic too." He said it was

OK and persuaded them to open the bag. 'Thank God,' I thought, and they found the bundle of medals on string. I made a joke, that if the plane was in trouble, I'd be handing these out to people and that even the pilot would get one. I have to smile now when I think about it; holding the queue up in the process, I had the uncanny knack of landing myself in trouble wherever I went. When my mom found out she said: "I told you so, and you must not go again." But I did.

I was with Blanche in Good Hope hospital when she was dying: she had pneumonia. I fetched the hospital Catholic chaplain to her, saying: "She's not a Catholic, but at one time she was having instructions in the faith with a priest from Coleshill and she never completed the course because she went into a nursing home out of town. On more than one occasion she said that she wanted to become a Catholic. Will you give her a special blessing, because she is a Christian, she used to attend the Anglican Church every week before she became infirm?" The priest asked Blanche if she wanted to be received into the church, because it could be arranged. She nodded, as she was too weak to talk and so he anointed her and she died a Catholic, which made me very happy. The priest told me that you have to be very careful not to impose that against someone's will and be absolutely sure that it was what he or she wanted. I told him: "I'm sure she will thank you one day for making it happen, even if it was on her deathbed. It's never too late."

That same priest sat down and wanted to chat; he told me that something extraordinary had happened to him that day at the hospital.

"What's that, Father?"

"Well, for the past few weeks, I've been ministering to an elderly Irish lady who died this morning. She was over here on holiday when she was taken ill, and we don't know who her relatives are to let them know what has happened. She told me that she belonged to the Third Order of St Francis and made me promise to see that she is buried in the brown habit of that order. I managed to get one for her and took it down to the morgue and left it there for her to be dressed in. I decided to take one last look at her and lifted up the sheet covering her face and I had a shock. I looked at her face and I tell you, if anyone had had a beatific vision she had, by the expression of ecstasy on her face. Her eyes and mouth were wide open and she looked so beautiful. I am convinced that because she was such a holy person, what she saw at the moment of her death was from Heaven."

"Oh, Father, what a pity you can't tell her family about that."

"Yes."

"Never mind, perhaps that sight was meant for your eyes only."

He nodded saying: "I think that's true."

Strangely, that priest was yet another to be called to the Lord. It seemed that I was meeting so many people who were here one day, and the next thing I heard was that they had passed away. This made me realise how short life can be: here today, gone tomorrow. Like my daughter, who died so young and so suddenly, I believe she knew that she wouldn't make old bones. She said that to me one day when I called in. She had been ill all that week with her asthma and I had been collecting her children from school. Roy used to go down to her house at night to help to put the children to bed – they loved the bedtime stories that he told them, just as he had done with his own children. He was a good father and now a wonderful grandfather to her children.

Caroline told me something else that day. As I was leaving she called me back.

"Mom."

"Yes love."

And with tears in her eyes she said: "I just want to say that you and dad have been real bricks lately, and I do love you.

Thanks." I had hugged her and told her we loved her too and that we were so proud of how she was coping on her own. "But you'll see, God will reward you for being a good mother to those children," I said. "I pray that later on some good man will come along and take care of you all, because you won't always have us, but while we're here we'll do our best. The only thing is, love, is that I'm so involved with the church, I think I'm going to resign because you need me now."

"No mom, don't – because I'm so proud of you and what your doing. Look how you consoled Mrs Murphy when her son died. Her daughter told me how much that meant to them. I'm going to tell you something else: you have prevented an abortion this week." Someone had told her that they were expecting their fourth baby and didn't want another child and was having a termination. That was until they saw my car come round the corner with a pro-life sticker on the rear window with the words: 'I'M GLAD JESUS'S MOTHER DIDN'T HAVE AN ABORTION'. "Seeing that changed her mind, mom. So look at the good your doing."

That baby was born after Caroline's death and the mother named it after Caroline. I remember that young woman was very upset at Caroline's funeral and I told her that she mustn't 'take on' so because it would affect her unborn baby. I got a phone call at 6am the day the baby was born, asking me to find a priest to come and baptise it because the baby was in trouble. I phoned Father Anton at home and woke him up. He got dressed quickly and met me at the maternity unit. Whilst Father Anton was baptising the infant in the incubator, I sat saying the rosary, I also prayed to our Caroline telling her to pray for her namesake here on earth. Thanks be to God, the baby pulled through, and is in senior school now.

I had to take the Pro Life sticker out of my car, because I had my car windows smashed in by pro-abortionists three times. I also had obscene graffiti painted all over my car when I was at Mass and another time, while at a Senatus meeting in St. Catherine's in the city, my windscreen was smashed, and the car was full of glass inside. The priest, Monsignor Fallon came in to tell me what had happened but I didn't jump up, I just continued on with the meeting and, after the final prayers, I went out with a brush and pan to clean up the mess. I wasn't ruffled, I was getting used to things like this happening and took it all in my stride: but I sure was being tried and tested.

The priest came out to give me a hand and said: "I've got to hand it to you, Pat, you don't let these things get you down do you."

"No, Father. It makes me think that I must be doing something really good to be punished like this."

"What do you mean?" he asked, looking puzzled.

"Don't you know, Father, that the more you love God and His Blessed Mother, the more the devil gets angry. I call this, 'Slaps in the face from Old Nick.' But he doesn't worry me, he will never win, because good overpowers evil every time."

"Very wise words, Pat," he said, as he helped me put a piece of cardboard down on the driver's seat in case I had missed some glass and sat on it. I drove home, stopping off at the nearest Auto-Glass centre to have the windscreen glass replaced.

I wasn't the only one being attacked like that. My elderly parish priest was being terrorised by youths, who climbed up onto his garage roof at night after he had gone to bed and banged on his bedroom wall with iron bars to wake him up. He confessed to us at Mass one morning that he was very tired, as he hadn't had any sleep all week with those little devils tormenting him. He was a nervous man and was afraid of these rascals. It's a sick world isn't it, with all the evil things that are going on? But just because the whole world is going mad, does not mean that we have to go mad with it.

Our Parish Church

*M*y eldest son Mark is a carpenter and he did lots of work for the church. Word got around among priests about his workmanship and he was kept very busy for a time. When his sister died, he decided to make a large wooden stable for the crib at Christmas for our church: 8ft by 6ft, big enough to house all the figures and animals inside. We put some straw down and a lantern inside to light it up, and the priest had a brass plaque made with Caroline's name on saying: 'Donated by the Brookes family, in memory of their daughter.' It has been used every Christmas for the past ten years, and every year it has been our job to erect and dismantle it. We also donated a chalice to hold the wine that becomes the Precious Blood in memory of our daughter and that also has her name inscribed on it, asking for prayers. We deem it a great honour to see her name on the chalice when we go up to receive Holy Communion.

There is a statue of Our Lady just inside the door of our parish church called, The Mother of God and Guardian Angels, which I gave to the church; although it badly needs painting, which I never get round to doing. I also donated a statue of St Joseph on the alter, both given to me by my missionary priest friend that came from his church in London that was sold. When I look around our church, I can see so many things that my family has had a hand in. The piety stall was built by my son, the wood panelling at the back of the church was fixed by my husband, the wooden partition window between the altar and the Lady Chapel was made and fitted by Mark. Roy designed and made the stained glass windows in the sacristy and the confessional box; and the family also made and fitted all the presbytery and meeting-room windows and doors. I used to make the altar cloths and small tablecloths. We also made and painted the wooden book barrow holding church magazines at the back of the church.

When you have lived in a parish for 45 years, you are bound to leave your mark, and we consider it a great privilege to work in God's house.

Another episode in my life was when I had alopecia and all my hair fell out. I think it was mainly caused through having no thyroid, as it is then that the hair tends to go thinner. One day my hairdresser noticed a small bald patch, about the size of a ten pence piece on the top of my head, but before long, I was completely bald with tufts of hair falling out overnight on my pillow. My doctor said it would come back on again, providing that I didn't lose my eyebrows – if that happened then the alopecia would be permanent. There are two types of alopecia: one where the hair grows back in a year or so, and the other where it never grows back. Every day I would examine my eyebrows; I still had them, but for 13 months I had to wear a wig. I bought a couple of good ones, the same colour as my own hair and read books on what foods to eat and helpful hints to make hair grow; vitamin B complex is recommended, so I ate brewer's yeast tablets by the handful.

I was upset at losing my nice long brown hair. My mother used to say: "Your hair is your crowning glory; don't cut it short." I never did, but I had no choice at that time. I would cry when I took the wig off at night, but I also thought: "Oh well, worse things happen, this is nothing compared to what I've had wrong with me in the past." I just tried to be patient and hope and pray that it would grow back, which it did, but it was not my natural colour at first. It grew back white initially, then gradually changed to brown.

Having alopecia helped make me realise what some people go through when they lose their hair after having chemotherapy. Meanwhile I would listen to women complaining about their hair and how they didn't know what to do with their 'mops' and secretly think: "Count yourself lucky to have hair at all." We take so many things for granted in our lives, and don't appreciate them until we lose them.

It wasn't until my mother died that I began to appreciate all that she did for me. I miss phoning her each day to tell her my troubles, and I have no-one to moan to now. Nobody understands you like your mom, and although I didn't take her advice about certain things because I was stubborn with a mind of my own and wouldn't be told what to do, I realise she had my best interests at heart and did love me in her own way.

When she was alive, I would phone her up every day and sometimes, when I was feeling down, she would buck me up, telling me not to lose heart, and say: "Where's your faith? Something will turn up just when you think you can't go on any longer, God lifts you up and sends help." This particular day I had read my horoscope in the newspaper, which I don't usually do as I don't believe in them, but what I read made me smile, and I related it to my mom.

"Funny you should say that, mom, because my stars say: 'Hang on. Help is on the way.' Well, I don't just need help, mom, I think it's going to take the cavalry to come to my rescue!" and we both laughed.

"That's it, love, never lose your sense of humour because if you can laugh in adversity, then all is not lost." Laugh, and the world laughs with you, cry and you cry alone.

Once, she gave me a competition to do, off the 'Daddies Sauce' bottle, saying; "You should do this love I reckon you'll win" and I did, I won first prize £1,000. And I shared it with her.

Mom died at 86. My brother John came over from Australia and my sister Carole came from Germany for her funeral; it was lovely to see them both after so many years. Our John was to give the eulogy on the altar about mom but he swears a lot – the Police force was to blame for that. I threatened him: "John, no swearing on the altar; remember where you are." He promised he wouldn't and, true to his word, he didn't. He did a good job but right at the end he finished off with: "Despite mom's hard life with many difficulties, she did her best; bloody well done, Mom."

Instead of it being a sad time because we had lost our mother, it was a joyous week, reminiscing about the past and our childhood: we laughed until we cried! Despite our separate lives, in different parts of the world, we had remained close: 'the family that prayed together, stayed together', even though thousands of miles kept us apart.

Three years before mom died, our youngest sister, Moira, died of ovarian cancer; she was only 51. Mom was devastated when that happened and I really think that she lost the will to live after that because she and Moira were inseparable. Moira was so brave. She kept her cancer a secret for four years until she got too ill to hide it.

When mom died it was sudden. I didn't have time to say goodbye, or be at her bedside saying the prayers for her and to thank her for my life. She was found six hours after she died, sitting on her toilet. She'd had a heart attack. I had seen her just three days before, when we visited as we did every week; she was very independent for her age, did all her own washing and cooking, and was very house-proud.

The same priest who had visited my sister in her last illness had continued visiting mom every week with the sacraments, and through him she became really devout. She told me that once, when he was giving her Holy Communion, she looked at him and saw Our Lord; he had such a good face. Another time when the priest called, she didn't want to let him in, because she had been baking cakes and her kitchen table was a mess with flour and pastry, but she realised that being house-proud took second place to receiving Jesus, because He didn't mind the state of the house, He was only interested in the state of the soul, and that is what we have to keep clean.

My brother-in-law Bill, who found her dead, phoned me. I said we would be down right away. When we got there the undertakers were also there to collect the body and they asked if I wanted to see her; of course I did. What a shock. I thought she would be laid out on the bed or on her settee but no, she was sitting upright in the middle of the floor. It upset me knowing that in order to get her into the body bag, they would have to break her legs to straighten her out. She also had her curlers in her hair, which I took out, knowing mom, she wouldn't like to be seen like that.

I phoned my brother and sister up and told them the sad news.

When we used to visit her, we always took her favourite meal of fish and chips. Roy did any odd jobs that needed doing and I tidied her garden and put some bedding plants around the borders. She loved her garden, she would sit on her bench and say: "God created us in a garden." Poor mom, I hope she's happy at last because she never was here on earth.

My greatest wish was that mom could forgive the hurts of the past and make her peace with my father. The first time I went to Lourdes I prayed for that and that they would become friends and bury the hatchet, (another minor miracle).

My dad was put in a nursing home before he passed away and I went up to Sheffield on the train to visit him a few times. The first time it was in December, around Christmas time. I took John-Paul with me, aged two, and when we got there the lady who showed us to his room said to John-Paul: "Have you come to see Father Christmas? He's in here" and opened the door.

My dad was sitting in an armchair wearing a red dressing gown with a big fluffy white beard and for all the world, you would swear that it was Father Christmas with his rosy red cheeks and twinkling blue eyes. I told my mother that he was a lonely old man now; it was sad how he had ended up. She said: "As you live, so you die. He has got out of life what he has put into it, which wasn't much." She said, she was so glad that she had stuck by us children all those years ago because we were all good kids; it made her feel humble thinking how good we were to her.

I was going to visit dad one time and out of the blue, mom said that she wanted to come with me. I thought it was only to gloat, but to my surprise, she was very kind towards him. She said to him: "Matt, do you remember when you used to sing that song to me that went something like this? (*I Dreamt I Walked in Marble Halls*) Well this is it, this house with its high glass domed ceilings and its marble hall and staircase." It had been a Lord's house years ago, before it was turned into an old people's home. My dad smiled, took her hand and together they walked hand-in-hand slowly up the stairs to his room. What a sight for sore eyes: it brought tears to mine anyway. They had made friends and buried the hatchet at last; my prayers had been answered.

The next time I visited him he seemed distant and changed towards me, as if he didn't know me any more. I thought he was going senile, but later I got a phone call from the home saying that he'd had a fall and broken his hip and was in hospital. As I was his next of kin, they needed my signature for the doctors to operate, so I went over to the hospital. When I arrived my dad had a terrible cold and chest infection. I spoke to his doctor saying: "Surely you're not going to operate on him in this condition, the anaesthetic will surely kill him?"

"Well let me put it like this, if we don't operate he will never walk again," the doctor said and he showed me the x-ray of his broken hip. I signed the consent form and he had the operation but I had signed his death warrant, because he got pneumonia and died without ever walking again.

I am glad I met up with him after all those years and told him that I had forgiven him; it would have been so much more pitiful if we hadn't had that short time together. I mustn't judge; God alone is the judge, He knows what's in the heart.

Missionaries

At home sometimes, I felt like the old woman who lived in the shoe, with so many children that I didn't know what to do. Our house was just like a hotel. I had a large house with a granny-flat extension to accommodate the grandchildren when they came to stay from Spain. The flat was also used to put up visiting legionaries from Dublin, and various missionaries. At one Senatus meeting I noticed two strangers sitting in the corner, one an old woman and the other a young girl. I was in charge of the refreshments that day and during the break went over to offer them something to eat. They seemed ravenous, as if they were starving. I asked them where they were from and they told me Australia. Because of my Australian connection I warmed to them immediately. They said that they were missionaries of St Benedict's order and had travelled all over the world for the last 11 years without any money whatsoever, just living on Providence and good people's help. I wondered how they could survive like that. They would need food, clothes, toiletries and other bits and pieces; no-one can survive without money, but they did. Apparently kind benefactors paid their fares wherever they went.

The older lady said her name was Mother Rose, and the young girl, about 18 years old, was called Rebecca.

"What's brought you here then?" I asked.

Mother Rose looked evasive and then said: "We are told where to go by the angels, and tonight we are coming home with you."

"No way." I thought, my husband is already complaining about all the waifs and strays I bring home – I dare not turn up with two more. Guess who ended up coming home for dinner and staying for a week? Yes, Mother Rose and Rebecca.

They said they wouldn't need much and it was just for one night. When the president announced in the meeting that we had two missionary ladies here who needed a bed for the night, I waited to see if anyone else offered, but no one did. I relented, and put my hand up. Once home, I realised that they couldn't leave with no money and nowhere to go. How could I refuse them help?

I had never met anyone like them before. They fasted all day Wednesday and Friday; I felt dreadful cooking meals for the family as they couldn't have any; it was their choice, but they both looked so thin and hungry. I secretly wondered if the old woman was eccentric and had some kind of hold over the young girl because the young girl seemed to be under her spell, almost too obedient.

I made their beds up but found the next morning they hadn't been slept in. Both Mother Rose and Rebecca had sat up all night, praying. I asked them: "Why, when you are both so tired?" They told me that they were guided to my house, which had needed a lot of prayers, because something was going to happen here and the prayers might avert it. I couldn't understand what they meant. Now, I started to think 'they are mad,' 'a pair of religious fanatics who tricked people into doing things for them'. I wasn't a fool.

Later, it became crystal clear that they must have been angels in disguise, who had been sent to help me because my daughter was going to die shortly. I couldn't understand why Mother Rose kept asking me about my daughter. "Caroline has asthma and her husband's left her with four young children. I'm very worried about her," I replied. Mother Rose nodded to confirm that she was in the right place.

I couldn't make them out, they were both very holy humble people who were homeless and I've always been a soft touch, but I didn't want them staying indefinitely. I asked where they were going next and they said 'Lourdes in France.' How could they with no money? After they had been staying a week, guess who paid their fares to Lourdes, hoping that some kind soul in Lourdes would see them on their way from there? My kindness cost me over £400 that visit, and that wasn't the end of it. They were back two or three times a year from then on, when they had nowhere to go and needed a bed. I fed them and clothed them then sent them on their way; each time they cleaned out my savings.

Rebecca told me that she needed a pair of shoes, as hers were worn out: she was a size larger than me or else I would have given her a pair of my own strong walking shoes but, they were too small so I took her shopping for a new pair. She picked a pair of men's hiking boots in her size, but when I saw the price I gasped. I had never paid that much for a pair of shoes in my life. I relented because she needed a strong pair, with all the walking they did – you only get what you pay for – and these would last her a long time.

Each time they were leaving they would take me to the travel agency or the bus station, and using their discount card, to get as much off the price of the trip as we could, I would pay for the tickets using my credit card. They never touched a penny themselves. I asked them where they got the discount card from and was told that a good man, named Michael in London, with whom they stayed sometimes, had bought it for them.

I couldn't afford to go on all these trips, yet somehow I was paying for these two strangers to travel the world. They did go to these places, because I would receive postcards from them, but how did they do it? I think I must have been under some spell believing that by helping them, I was helping the many others they helped, because in my eyes they were doing good.

The young girl played the violin and carried it around with her everywhere.

On one of their visits, Mother Rose said she had to go to give a talk at the seminary and wanted the phone number of Oscott College. To my amazement, the dean of the college agreed for her to give a talk to the students; I went with her as her driver. I suppose they wanted her to give the talk because she was a missionary, and some of the young students to the priesthood would be going to different missionary posts abroad. I had no idea what she was going to say to them but she was quite stern with them, she told them that if they didn't intend being good holy priests then to pack their bags and leave right now and get out. Then she told them something along the same lines that St Maximilian Kolbe once said to a group of newly ordained priests many years before. St Maximilian Kolbe was the priest who died in a concentration camp during World War II, having sacrificed his life so that another prisoner, who had a family, could go free. (Greater love hath no man than to lay down his life for his friends). Mother Rose gave the young students that same pep talk saying:

> "In your lives as priests, there will be periods of darkness when you'll get discouraged and deterred from your faith, but discouragement is the tool of the devil. Satan does not sleep, he will often suggest to you that there are other joys of life that you could be taking part in, instead of doing God's work, but those who really love Our Lady are quick to recognise the enemy within and repel him, and by offering our temptations and difficulties to Mary we will always gain victory, and of course prayer is the greatest weapon that we have against discouragement. If there were no trials to bear, and no struggle, victory would be impossible. Without victory there is no crown, no reward, for what, would we go to heaven for?
> In our religious lives we must be careful not to imitate

bad example, remembering that even amongst the Apostles there was a Judas. We should only imitate the best, and work with greater effort every day to please God. Always remember that you are God's chosen sons; good priests can save many souls but a bad priest can lose souls, and deter people from their faith.

You have been chosen to do God's work on earth and you should be proud that you have been chosen, yet humble enough to realise that you can do nothing without God so never get above your station, you are here to serve and save souls."

I thought it was a lovely pep talk, considering she was in her eighties and very poorly with a chest infection at the time. Before leaving the house, I had been trying to dose her up with flu medicines; I even told her not to go because she wasn't well enough, but she was adamant that she must go; she was on a special mission.

I have met some wonderful people. I started to believe that maybe Mother Rose was sent by the angels to different places to do good, because I sensed that she was doing good there that night. At least she gave those young men something to think about.

I remember one day I had to take those missionaries to the bus station in Digbeth. They were off on their travels again, this time to London. I drove round for a while trying to find a parking space; it was before the new station was built with a car park. I eventually found somewhere to park nearby, outside some offices, and duly parked up and saw them off on the coach. When I returned to my car it had been clamped and there was a sticker on the windscreen. I phoned the number on the piece of paper and within seconds a white van pulled up alongside me with two men inside. They wanted £80 to unclamp it. I didn't have any money on me but the men said that they would drive me to the nearest cash-point to get it.

(This is what I get for doing a good turn). I hadn't seen any 'No Parking' notices, but they pointed one out to me, high up on the wall of the office building, too high up for anyone in a car to notice. What a scam! I had just enough in the bank to pay the fine. They released the clamp and I drove home thinking: 'Another fine mess', I'm getting fed up with this.'

Later on, I read in the newspaper that other people who had been clamped in that same place had taken the company to court and had their money refunded. I should have done that.

I don't know what became of those two missionaries because they stopped coming some years ago. Maybe Mother Rose died. I asked her once: "Aren't you tired of roaming the world with no fixed abode?" and she replied: "Jesus had nowhere to lay his head, but one day please God, I will lay down for good in some nice convent that will take us in." I hope she got her wish, and I hope Rebecca has made a nice life for herself.

My Retirement

For six years after Caroline died I struggled to continue in the Legion; but my heart wasn't in it as much. I kept thinking of my mom's old saying: 'A bird can sing with a broken wing but not with a broken heart,' and Roy my husband had become a broken man. He had just had a knee replacement because of arthritis and had to retire early from work; he actually recovered quite well from the operation and it was a great success. Two years later, I plucked up my courage to have the same operation. I was in so much pain that I would scream out walking or climbing stairs, and as Roy was doing so well with his new knee, I decided that I had no choice if I wanted to walk without pain. It's a pity that my poor grandmother couldn't have had the same operation because she suffered untold agony with her arthritic knees.

Shortly after I resigned from the Legion I had my knee replacement surgery; unfortunately it wasn't successful. For 18 months after the operation I attended the fracture clinic for check ups, each time expressing my concern that something was wrong as I was still in a lot of pain. I couldn't understand it – I had done all the exercises faithfully, even had hydrotherapy in the heated pool twice a week.

The doctors kept saying: "Give it another month or two and you'll be free of pain." The x-rays were all perfect, according to them, and there was no reason why I should be in pain. I am sure they didn't believe me. In the meantime, I was getting hooked on the painkillers they were giving me, which made me so constipated and dopey, but didn't help much, I began to think that perhaps I shouldn't have had it done because with no thyroid, my own GP had warned that the bones might not heal as they should. But it wasn't that.

When it came time for me to be discharged from hospital, I happened to see a different surgeon and he sent me down for one last x-ray. I remember my leg was swollen, and so stiff I had difficulty straightening it up so that I could stand in front of the x-ray machine. I had the x-ray taken and took it back to the doctor to have a look at.

"Tell me, Mrs Brookes, are you still in a lot of pain?"

"Yes I am, and I am not happy with the way it's gone."

"Well, I can see the problem," said the doctor.

"Thank God," I said, "because I haven't been telling lies. I'm no stranger to suffering but this is very bad, doctor."

"I'm not surprised," he said.

"For some reason the surgeon who performed your operation has left a part out."

"What!" I exclaimed.

He hesitated, as if he didn't want to get the surgeon into trouble. "For some reason he omitted to put the silicone cushion that stops the metal rubbing on the kneecap, round the metal implant. Consequently, instead of bone rubbing on bone, as you had before, you now have metal rubbing on bone. We can open you up and do it all over again."

"Oh no. I can't go through all that again. I had an aunt who had that done and she ended up in a wheelchair."

"Ah yes, there is a risk of that happening because we could damage the kneecap in the process of getting it off again."

I became annoyed, saying: "I wouldn't let you lot touch me again. Especially as you have been lying to me for two years, saying my other x-rays were perfect and that I was imagining it. You can discharge me. I'll have to resign myself to being in pain for the rest of my life, thanks to this hospital!" I threatened them with my solicitor but never actually followed it up; I should have sued them for their incompetence and the suffering they've caused me.

Having resigned from the Legion because of my arthritis and with my mother not well, I felt rather defeated, but I knew my priorities and that Our Lady would understand. I would still do good works in different ways; my path had just taken a different course now, leaving me to concentrate on my husband and family. I always looked forward to the time when we could do things together before it was too late; She has granted us a happy retirement, after being in her service for 20 years.

Celebrations

Roy and I both celebrated our 70th birthdays, one after another, with surprise parties at our David's house, and for our Golden Wedding Anniversary, the family paid for us to have a lovely holiday in Torquay. This is what I had been missing. We have always been close, Roy and I, and these twilight years are bringing us closer then ever and I am very grateful to have this time with my husband still with me.

We plan to go to Australia in the near future to visit my brother John and his wife Mary, as they are always asking us to go for a holiday and it would be nice to visit some of the places we used to know. I think I could tolerate the climate better now, so – please God – we will do that one-day. But before that, we were able to see our son, John-Paul, get married in May 2011 to a lovely girl, Donna. I used to pray to Our Lady to guide him to find a good wife, so when he brought this girl home who he had known from school, and who also happens to be a Catholic, I was delighted, particularly when I found out that her name meant 'Lady'. I thought that meant one Lady had found another lady for my son.

As for our surprise birthday parties, I didn't know I had such devious children and grandchildren. It was Roy's birthday first; our David had planned the surprise party months before. I had to be in on that, but I kept the secret. The family said they were more surprised that I was able to keep that secret from Roy, because he really was astonished, and thoroughly enjoyed every minute of it.

We decided to make Roy's party fancy dress and as Roy has always loved cowboy films, we chose a western theme. David had bought him a sheriff's outfit complete with cowboy hat and guns to wear. Julie, David's wife, is a chef, and often invites us over for a nice meal, so we used that as our excuse to get him there. Roy could never refuse one of Julie's meals, so when she phoned him up saying: "I'm cooking something special for your birthday, " (which wasn't a lie), he said OK, what time?"

" 7:30," replied Julie.

I told them we couldn't be there any earlier than that because we would be at Saturday evening Mass first and would go on from there. Everyone else had to be at David's house for 7 o'clock. Little did Roy know that underneath my coat in church I was wearing my cowgirls outfit. I had given my hat to David earlier to keep at his house.

Mass finished early that night and off we set, but realising that we would be there too early and everyone might not have arrived, I had to make some excuse to delay us. First of all I said: "Stop at the shop for a bunch of flowers for Julie, in appreciation for the meal." I was ages in the shop while he was waiting in the car. I was trying to kill time; I came out with the flowers. Then as we were near David's road, I said: "Stop the car," (thinking we were still too early and could bump into people going into the house, which would give the game away).

"What for now?" Roy asked.

"I have awful indigestion and I need to get some ginger ale from that off-licence." He tutted and waited in the car while I went into the shop – I was telling lies now. I came out with a bottle of Dry Ginger in a brown paper bag. Roy wound his car window down saying: "You look just like 'Wino Lil.' Get in the car before anyone sees you."

About 40 people were at the party all dressed up as 'Cowboys (or cowgirls) and Indians'. Mark was 'Big Chief Sitting Bull' and wore a big-feathered headdress; David was 'Wyatt Earp'; Julie a saloon girl; and even the children had their hair in plaits with a feather in, just like little squaws.

The planning that went into that party made it all the more special. Julie had really excelled herself with all the food; she had even done hot chilli and beans as well as the cold buffet. They had hired a 'Bucking Bronco Bull' for the children to go on, with a prize for the one who could stay on the longest. There was also a shooting game, to see who was the quickest on the draw when a cardboard cowboy figure burst out through saloon doors.

Everyone enjoyed it so much; Roy has played the video of it over and over again, remembering all the fun we had. David and Julie had worked so hard preparing it all that when it was coming up to my birthday, the following year, I made them promise that we would all go out for a nice meal at a restaurant instead, as I didn't want to put them through all that trouble again. I thought I had made it quite clear that I didn't want a big party for my birthday – but they fooled me.

Three days before my birthday it was one of our great granddaughter's third birthday and I thought we were going to her party. We turned up with a card and present, and I was genuinely shocked when I arrived to find even more guests waiting for me to arrive.

"You devious lot," I said. "I didn't think much would get past my eyes but it really did this time."

On our way there I happened to say to Roy: "I'm glad we are going to the casino for my birthday, and that David and Julie are not planning anything else….they're not are they? I hope they are not trying to pull the wool over my eyes like they did with you."

"Don't be daft," said Roy, "you know you're going for a meal on Wednesday. Don't be greedy, you cant have both." That had shut me up, but in fact I had a wonderful surprise party at David's house and because it was already booked, the family all came to the casino on the actual day as well.

As before, it was fancy dress with everyone in costumes

from the 1950s. 'Rock and Rollers', 'Elvis Presley', 'Marilyn Monroe'. David was dressed as 'Buddy Holly' and a few of the men were the 'Blues Brothers', dressed all in black with dark sunglasses. The granddaughters were all in spotted flared skirts and wearing blonde wigs. Roy was dressed up as a 'Teddy Boy'; I'm so glad they waited until he got there to dress him up because as before, we had come from church and if he was dressed in a bright shiny-blue 'Teddy Boy's' outfit, with drainpipe trousers in church, we would never have lived it down.

Julie took me up into the bedroom and said: "Try this on, mom." Julie and Aleshia were dressing me up in a 1950s, flared frilly dress, just like the ones I used to have in my teens, when Roy and I used to go dancing. It was a tight-fitting Lycra top and showed up all my bulges! They took some photos of Roy and I together; we looked like the 'Oldest Swingers in Town'.

Photos of me at different ages were posted around the room; our David came in with a big red book like, Eamonn Andrews used to have in, 'This is Your Life' on TV and read out all the events of my life. Halfway through he put the television on to play two CDs, one off my brother, John, and one off my sister, Carole, wishing me a 'Happy Birthday'.

John was really comical, saying in his Australian accent: "Now sweetheart, if you have got any priest friends present, get them to anoint you straight away because it says in the Bible that once you have reached three-score-years-and-ten then you have had your lot, so don't delay."

David has a large house but to accommodate all the people he had put a large marquee in his big back garden; it must have cost them a fortune. A jukebox was playing all the 'Rock and Roll' music and just as before, Julie had put on a lovely spread. I'll never forget that night, realising how much my family loves me; even those who live up north and long distances away came. Everyone enjoyed both the parties so much, they all want to know when the next one is – I think poor David and Julie would probably have a breakdown with all the hard work. They both had to have a week off work before the parties, as there was so much preparation that went into them.

Our Mark had helped by making stalls and fixtures illustrating events in our lives, like for example a huge picture of a ship painted on a board and behind it a sign saying, 'Tilbury Docks', then another sign saying 'This way to the car-boot sale,' with an actual table with bric-a-brac on it, which was for my benefit as they knew how much I loved car-boot sales.

The night before, Mark had been missing when I'd cooked him a meal and I had told him off when he eventually got back, saying: "Where have you been?"

"David's," he replied, but what I didn't know was that he was working hard, getting things ready for the party and helping David with last-minute preparations.

I am so blessed with such a loving family, and to think that when David was born I nearly lost him.

Our seventieth year was very eventful because as well as parties and a holiday, both Roy and I received the 'Ubi Caritas' medal for our services to the church, with a certificate signed by the Bishop. Another milestone in our lives.

The Conclusion

Looking back, I am thankful for a wonderful life: one that has been so full and blessed. I feel I am loved so much and will never be lonely because with such a big family, and lovely friends there is never a dull moment. There have been many parties over the years at our house, making up for all the time that we didn't have birthday parties as children or were never allowed to bring friends home.

I have been toying with the idea of what to call this book and decided to call it, *All for the Love of Our Lady* because I have lived all my life doing just that, and She has held my hand in so many difficulties. Friends and neighbours have always said that whatever befalls me, even tragedies, I have managed to get over them and bounce back. I always reply: "That's because somebody up there loves me and I trust in them."

Whatever happens, this book will be a legacy to leave to my children and grandchildren, because the greatest thing I can pass down to them is my most treasured possession, my Catholic faith. I must tell you that I have not done this on my own. I have sensed help along the way, and because this book is about my life, the episodes have been recalled with ease and every word is true. I have also encountered obstacles along the way, meant to deter me, especially when the computer kept playing up and deleting dozens of pages after I had typed them, but this is the story of someone who doesn't give up when things go wrong, and who trusts in God to see her through.

Even though I am not in the Legion of Mary any more, I am still a Legionary at heart, and still distribute Her medal to anyone who needs it. For instance, a few weeks ago I had an occasion to buy a new car – a second-hand car, but newer than our old one. Our grandson, who is a mechanic and deals in cars, told us about a car he had seen online, which was a real bargain, with low mileage on the clock and looking brand new. He took us to see it; we fell in love with it and bought it. The young man who was selling it told us that he had a brain tumour and his driving licence had been taken off him so he couldn't drive anymore. Well, as you might guess, I gave him one of my medals, along with four more for his wife and three children. He has since had the tumour removed and is now having radiotherapy treatment; I am praying for that man and trusting in Our Lady to help him recover. I believe that the people we meet are put in our path for a reason.

It is no coincidence that I met this man because he needed encouraging words to lift him up and give him hope. I told him to think positive, and positive things will happen, just like they did for me when I had cancer over 30 years ago.

It takes one who has suffered to really feel for another going though the same thing; cancer is a terrible disease where you feel so alone and all at sea. Totally at the mercy of others, but no-one can help more than you can help yourself, with the right attitude and not giving in to it; your faith can make you whole again. I used to talk to my body and tell the cancer to be gone, that I didn't want it, it was alien to me so, I said: "Get lost." I read books on self-help. I tried everything: eating anything green I could lay my hands on, even grass out of the garden, which was just like eating cress on a salad. Green vegetables have great healing properties and grapes get rid of toxins in the body. I remember reading that one lady cured herself of lung disease by eating copious amounts of grapes every day. There must be some truth in the benefits of eating grapes, as we are encouraged to take them to the sick in hospital.

My youngest son, John-Paul, had a beautiful wedding and

everything was perfect, including the weather. The bride looked stunning, so did the bridesmaids and the reception was great, with some 300 guests. Quite a few of us stayed overnight at the hotel and, 'a wonderful time was had by all.' The happy couple went on honeymoon to Hawaii.

At the wedding, I looked around and considered myself so blessed with such a wonderful family, who all love each other and get on so well. I realised that this is something rare today. Our family is still growing, with more members to fit in the jigsaw and I hope and pray there will be more to come. Thank you, Lord for letting me live to see all this. Every time I say the Magnificat prayer it becomes personal when I repeat Our Lady's words: "He who is mighty has done great things to me, and Holy is His name.

We have recently found out that we are to become grandparents again next March as John-Paul and Donna are expecting their first baby.

Recently, at Mass, our parish priest's sermon was about how Jesus chose His Apostles from all walks of life; they were the most unlikely bunch of people to help Him. They were not learned scholars, mainly simple fishermen. The priest said: "Have you ever heard of the saying, 'You can't make a silk purse out of a sow's ear?' Well Jesus could, and He did with those men." I think that He's also done that with me.

If this book helps someone to discover the power of prayer and trust in God, then my life will not be in vain. Prayer is mightier than an Atom Bomb, because it's so far reaching and so powerful; it can change the course of events, alleviate suffering and avert disasters. No matter what crosses we have to bear in life, prayer can help in that too, making the crosses easier to bear. Remember though, that the sufferings of this life are nothing compared to the joys that are to come in the next, and that by offering our sufferings up, we are gaining graces and merits for Heaven.

The End